BIOENGINEERING

EDITED BY ELIZABETH LACHNER

Britannica®
Educational Publishing
IN ASSOCIATION WITH

ROSEN
EDUCATIONAL SERVICES

First Edition

Britannica Educational Publishing
J.E. Luebering: Director, Core Reference Group

Rosen Publishing
Hope Lourie Killcoyne: Executive Editor
Amelie von Zumbusch: Editor
Nelson Sá: Art Director
Brian Garvey: Designer
Cindy Reiman: Photography Manager

Library of Congress Cataloging-in-Publication Data

Bioengineering/edited by Elizabeth Lachner.—First edition.
    pages cm.—(The biotechnology revolution)
Includes bibliographical references and index.
ISBN 978-1-62275-580-6 (library bound)
1. Bioengineering—Juvenile literature. 2. Biotechnology—Juvenile literature. I. Lachner, Elizabeth, editor.
TA164.B45 2015
660.6—dc23

2014047675

Manufactured in the United States of America

Photo credits: Cover, p. 1 anyaivanova/Shutterstock.com; pp. viii–ix Bloomberg/Getty Images; p. 5 © JPC-PROD/Fotolia; p. 11 Leonard Lee Rue III/Science Source/Getty Images; pp. 14, 42, 68, 79, 84, 107, 146, 150, 161 Encyclopædia Britannica, Inc.; p. 18 Keith Brofsky/Photodisc/Thinkstock; p. 25 serts/E+/Getty Images; pp. 32–33 kristian sekulic/E+/Getty Images; pp. 38–39 monkeybusinessimages/iStock/Thinkstock; pp. 44–45, 112 BSIP/UIG/Getty Images; p. 49 Walter Reed/U.S. Army; p. 58 Hank Morgan/Science Source/Getty Images; p. 60 Apogee/Science Source; pp. 64–65 Burger/Phanie/Science Source; p. 72 Scott Camazine/Science Source/Getty Images; p. 89 Magan-Domingo/age fotostock/Getty Images; pp. 94–95, 114–115, 134 Science Source; p. 99 James King-Holmes/Science Source; p. 124 Tom Deerinck and Mark Ellisman of the National Center for Microscopy and Imaging Research at the University of California at San Diego; p. 140 © huimin/Fotolia; p. 154 © Aerial Achives/Alamy; cover and interior design elements vitstudio/Shutterstock.com (DNA), everythingpossible/iStock/Thinkstock (honeycomb), style_TTT/Shutterstock.com (linear patterns).

CONTENTS

INTRODUCTION

In 2013, bioengineers from Cornell University and physicians from Weill Cornell Medical College published a study describing how they were able to use a 3-D printer to produce artificial ears that look and act like real ears. The team, lead by Lawrence Bonassar and Dr. Jason Spector, fed a 3-D image of a human ear to a 3-D printer, which was able to use the image to create a mold of a human external ear. They filled the mold with collagen that came from rat tails, which provided a framework on which cartilage cells—from cow ears—that were then added could grow. In the future, the team hopes to be able to use human cartilage cells grown in a lab in the place of ones from cows. The plan is that these artificial ears could be used on children who are born with microtia, a congenital deformity in which the external ear does not fully develop. The artificial ears could also potentially be used to replace external ears that were lost to cancer or in accidents.

Scientists are also experimenting with various techniques to grow artificial human skin. An international team headed by Dr. Theodora Mauro, from San Francisco Veteran Affairs Medical Center, and Dr. Dusko Ilic, from King's College London, announced in 2014 that it had used stem cells to grow 1-centimetre (.39-inch) wide patches of epidermis, as the outer layer of human skin is known. The samples had the same properties as normal human skin. The scientists hope that the epidermis fragments could be used to test medicines and cosmetics. This would avoid the need for testing on animals, which can be less accurate than testing on humans and is a controversial procedure, banned in some areas.

While these accomplishments are impressive, they're just the latest in a long line of incredible advances that have been made over the last century. Take, for example, the first implant of an artificial lens in a human eye, which was made by Dr. Harold Ridley on Nov. 27, 1947, at London's Saint Thomas Hospital. While treating Royal Air Force (RAF) pilots during World War II, Ridley had noticed that when small pieces of PPMA (a certain kind of plastic that was used for the windshields and cupolas of RAF planes) got into the pilots' eyes after plane crashes, the pilots' eyes did not reject them. This got him thinking about how the same material could be used to make artificial lenses to replace damaged ones.

All of these impressive efforts are examples of bioengineering at work. Bioengineering is the application of engineering knowledge to the fields of medicine and biology. The bioengineer must

Bioengineers at Sapphire Energy, Inc., in San Diego, Calif., use cultivated algae to produce crude oil, lessening the need for oil drilling.

be well grounded in biology and have engineering knowledge that is broad, drawing upon electrical, chemical, mechanical, and other engineering disciplines. The bioengineer may work in any of a large range of areas. One of these is the provision of artificial means to assist defective body functions — such as hearing aids, artificial limbs, and supportive or substitute organs. In another direction, the bioengineer may use engineering methods to achieve biosynthesis of animal or plant products—such as for fermentation processes.

Let's take a closer look at the two elements of the word "bioengineering." The prefix "bio" indicates something having to do with life or living organisms, as is evident in the word "biology," meaning the study of living things and their vital processes. Biology deals with all the physicochemical aspects of life. The basic principles of biology include homeostasis (that all living things maintain a constant internal environment), unity (that all living organisms, regardless of their uniqueness, have certain biological, chemical, and physical characteristics in common), evolution (that the various types of plants, animals, and other living things on Earth have their origin in other preexisting types and that the distinguishable differences are due to modifications in successive generations), diversity (that, despite the basic biological, chemical, and physical similarities found in all living things, a diversity of life exists not only among and between species but also within every natural population), interrelationship (that living things have an impact on each other and on their environment), and continuity (that the ability to reproduce is one of the most important characteristics of life).

Engineering is the application of science to the optimum conversion of the resources of nature to the uses of humankind. The field has been defined by the Engineers Council for Professional Development as the creative application of "scientific principles to design or develop structures, machines, apparatus, or manufacturing processes, or works utilizing them singly or in combination; or to construct or operate the same with full cognizance of their design; or to forecast their behaviour under specific operating conditions; all as respects an intended function, economics of operation and safety to life and property." Associated with engineering is a great body of special knowledge; preparation for professional practice involves extensive training in the application of that knowledge. Standards of engineering practice are maintained through the efforts of professional societies, usually organized on a national or regional basis, with each member acknowledging a responsibility to the public over and above responsibilities to his employer or to other members of his society.

The function of the scientist is to know, while that of the engineer is to do. The scientist adds to the store of verified, systematized knowledge of the physical world; the engineer brings this knowledge to bear on practical problems. Engineering is based principally on physics, chemistry, and mathematics and their extensions into materials science, solid and fluid mechanics, thermodynamics, transfer and rate processes, and systems analysis.

While there is a real difference in emphasis between biology and bioengineering, it's also worth remembering that the two fields have significant overlap. In fact, bioengineering is a truly interdisciplinary field, drawing on the techniques and knowledge of all branches of science and engineering. Bioengineering draws so much from related fields, it can be difficult to know where bioengineering ends and those other fields—such as biochemistry or materials engineering—begin. This confusion is furthered by the fact that bioengineering is a fairly new and quickly evolving field. Incorporating knowledge or techniques from disciplines—some of which may seem only tangentially related to bioengineering—has led to the creation of myriad subfields of bioengineering; some of those subfields, such as genetic engineering, have become major fields in their own right.

While the murky borders between bioengineering and its related fields stir up some confusion, the differing ways in which the term "bioengineering" is used sow even more confusion. The term is often used as a synonym for "biomedical engineering" or "medical engineering." Medical engineering concerns the application of engineering principles to medical problems specifically, including the replacement of damaged organs, instrumentation, and diagnostic applications of computers. Others use a broader definition of the term "bioengineering," encompassing areas such as agricultural engineering, bionics, biochemical engineering, environmental engineering, human-factors engineering, and genetic engineering, seeing that these all have to do with the application of engineering principles to living things. This volume uses the latter, more expansive definition. That said, there is a particularly strong focus on biomedical engineering, in part because some people do use the stricter definition that narrows bioengineering to biomedical engineering and in part because of the wealth of amazing advances that have been made in that area over the last century.

Before World War II the field of bioengineering was essentially unknown, and little communication or interaction existed between the engineer and the life scientist. A few exceptions, however, should be noted. Agricultural engineers and chemical engineers who study fermentation processes are bioengineers in the broadest sense of the definition since they deal with biological systems. The civil engineer, specializing in sanitation, has also applied biological principles. Mechanical engineers have worked with the medical profession for many years in the development of artificial limbs. Another area of mechanical engineering that falls in the field of bioengineering is the air-conditioning field. In the early 1920s engineers and physiologists were employed by the American Society of Heating and Ventilating Engineers to study the effects of temperature and humidity on humans and to provide design criteria for heating and air-conditioning systems.

Today there are many more examples of inter-action between biology and engineering, particularly in the medical and life-support fields. In addition to an increased awareness of the need for communica-tion between the engineer and the associate in the life sciences, there is an increasing recognition of the role the engineer can play in several of the biological fields, including human medicine, and, likewise, an awareness of the contributions biological science can make toward the solution of engineering problems.

Much of the increase in bioengineering activity can be credited to electrical engineers. In the 1950s bioengineering meetings were dominated by sessions devoted to medical electronics. Medical instrumen-tation and medical electronics continue to be major areas of interest, but biological modeling, blood-flow dynamics, prosthetics, biomechanics (dynamics of body motion and strength of materials), biological heat transfer, biomaterials, and other areas are now included in conference programs.

Bioengineering developed out of specific desires or needs: the desire of surgeons to bypass the heart, the need for replacement organs, the requirement for life support in space, and many more. In most cases the early interaction and education were a result of personal contacts between physician, or physiologist, and engineer. Communication between the engineer and the life scientist was immediately recognized as a problem. Most engineers who wandered into the field in its early days probably had an exposure to biology through a high-school course and no further work. To overcome this problem, engineers began to study not only the subject matter but also the methods and techniques of their counterparts in medicine, physiology, psychology, and biology. Much of the information was self-taught or obtained through personal association and discussions. Finally, recognizing a need to assist in overcoming the communication barrier as well as to prepare engineers for the future, engineering schools developed courses and curricula in bioengineering.

CHAPTER 1

BIOLOGICAL CONTROL SYSTEMS

W alking and talking, seeing and hearing, grasping and throwing, and many other common actions are so much a part of everyday life that few people give them much thought. However, scientists who work in the field of bioengineering—including biologists, physicists, engineers, and physicians—study in great detail the biological control systems that regulate these everyday actions. Without knowing how biological control systems operate, bioengineers could not devise artificial body parts that function in practically the same way as natural ones.

REGULATING LIVING THINGS

Living things, like mechanical engines, need regulators for effective operation. The regulators of living things are called biological control systems. Among the many control systems are the ones that maintain a balance in the biophysical and biochemical functioning of the body, keep internal body temperature at a stable level in all kinds of weather, and regulate eye movements in visual tracking.

The analysis of any control system—biological or technological—requires a knowledge of its information flow. In diagramming information flow, the analyst strips away detailed physical descriptions of the system under study and notes only the flow of information essential to its operation. For example, someone learning to drive a car must understand the relationship between the position of the accelerator and the motion of the vehicle but does not need to know the sequence of spark plug firing in the engine.

HOMEOSTASIS

Many homeostatic biological control systems are at work in the body. Homeostasis is the stable operation of physiological activities. It is established by the receptor cells, which sense and report important environmental signals and body conditions; the neurons, or nerve cells, which transmit and process information; and the muscle cells, which exert force and produce movement.

All body cells, whatever their function, must have a supply of oxygen and food and be capable of responding to directions from hormones and other controls. All body cells must also be able to get rid of heat and such metabolic wastes as carbon dioxide. The blood enables the cells to perform these functions. The blood distribution system has a network of about a billion capillaries. Each of the billions of cells in the human body is close enough to a capillary to exchange materials, energy, and information with it. However, for the cells to operate efficiently, the temperature and pressure of the blood plasma that bathes them must be held within narrow ranges.

The biological control system for homeostasis is similar to the one for eye movement control. For homeostasis, however, the desired conditions do not vary but remain at set points, and system disturbances rather than changing targets of vision provide the input for feedback control. Among the important homeostatic systems of the body are the ones that regulate blood pressure, blood cell production, blood sugar, and metabolism.

BLOOD PRESSURE

The body monitors blood pressure by means of receptors in the main arteries from the heart. The body controls blood pressure through changes in heartbeat and the flow of blood through the heart. Blood pressure can also be regulated by vasomotor effectors that increase or decrease the diameter of particular blood vessels. Physical exertion and the digestion of food place heavy demands on the heart's blood output, which can be increased as much as ten-fold to meet such special needs. Despite these extreme changes in blood flow, homeostatic controls keep the variations in blood pressure within a relatively narrow range, barring disease or disorders.

BLOOD CELL PRODUCTION

Red blood cells pick up oxygen in lung capillaries and deliver it throughout the body. Because these cells function for only about three months, they must be replaced continually. White blood cells attack and destroy invading cells and other undesirable matter. The varying quantity of white blood cells required to perform these functions is regulated by homeostatic mechanisms.

BLOOD SUGAR

Glucose, a type of sugar, is the main energy source of cells. The maintenance of a balanced blood-sugar level ordinarily depends on the ability of the liver to make sugar when the supply on hand is inadequate. Insulin, a hormone made in the pancreas, helps transfer blood sugar into the cells. When this system breaks down, the body is unable to produce the full amount of insulin needed by the homeostatic blood-sugar mechanisms, resulting in a serious disease called diabetes mellitus.

In diabetes an example is seen of the rather narrow ranges in which homeostasis operates, since either an inadequate or an excessive supply of insulin can cause unconsciousness.

METABOLISM

Although people may take in several times their weight in food each year, their weight usually does not fluctuate much. This is another example of homeostasis. The food that is eaten is converted into energy or into replacement material for the body. Homeostatic metabolic controls regulate the distribution of the varying quantity of energy sources needed

People with diabetes must check their blood glucose levels regularly, as this young man is doing. Injections of insulin are used to maintain healthy blood glucose levels.

within the body. Leg muscles, for example, may briefly generate as much as one horsepower. By contrast, the basal metabolic rate for the entire body is only about 0.1 horsepower. (A basal metabolic rate is a measure of the total biological activity of a body at complete rest.)

CONSERVATION IN HOMEOSTATIC SYSTEMS

Every homeostatic system utilizes some principle of conservation. The total matter and energy of the system as a whole does not change. However, that is not the case for particular parts of the system. A familiar mechanical example, the flow of liquids through pipes, may make clear why this is so. If a liquid is piped into a storage compartment at certain flow rates and piped out at other rates, then, by the principle that all liquid is conserved, the net difference equals the rate of storage. The outflow rates usually depend on the height of the stored liquid, and through the use of feedback controls the inflow rates can be regulated by the height of the stored liquid. For example, the refill rate of a toilet tank depends on the gap between the desired and the existing water level. As the tank float rises, this gap is closed. When the required level is reached a valve shuts off the incoming water.

A homeostatic system may be regarded as a combination of several interconnected "pipes" and "compartments." Its "flow rates" are related to physiological equivalents of compartmental "heights," such as chemical concentrations, pressures, and temperatures.

Closed-loop control, so called because it has a feedback pathway, is cumbersome for simple repeated tasks. In the course of a lifetime, various limb and eye movements must be repeated millions of times. If open-loop programs lacking feedback are developed for these common actions, reflex actions not requiring the unnecessary processing of information become possible. Open-loop programs are somewhat like a fixed set of menu choices at a cafeteria. Anyone who eats there regularly can place an order without bothering to analyze the menu.

THERMOREGULATION

Nearly all energy from food and other sources leaves the body as heat. Thus, the body needs a well-functioning homeostatic control system for thermal regulation. Enzyme-controlled biochemical reactions in the body are usually most efficient at around 98° F (37° C). This temperature is the average set point for the inner body temperature of mammals. Cold-blooded animals, lacking a set body temperature, are prisoners of their environment. Snakes, for instance, must crawl under rocks and remain inactive during periods of extreme heat. When the temperature drops too low, they become sluggish. Mammals, by contrast, can live actively almost anywhere on Earth at almost any time.

In thermoregulation, the "flow rate" of body heat is related to the "heights" of such "compartments" as the

POIKILOTHERMY AND HOMOIOTHERMY

Also called cold-bloodedness, ectothermy, or heterothermy, poiki-lothermy is the state of having a variable body temperature that is usually only slightly higher than the environmental temperature. This state distinguishes fishes, amphibians, reptiles, and invertebrate animals from warm-blooded, or homoiothermic, animals. Because of their dependence upon environmental warmth for metabolic functioning, the distribution of terrestrial cold-blooded animals is limited, with only a few exceptions, to areas with a temperature range of 5–10° to 35–40° C (41–50° to 95–104° F). For cold-blooded animals living in the arctic seas, temperatures may range from below 0° C to 10–15° C (below 32° F to 50–59° F). Poikilotherms do maintain a limited control over internal temperature by behavioral means, such as basking in sunlight to warm their bodies.

The ability to maintain a relatively constant internal tempera-ture (about 37° C [99° F] for mammals, about 40° C [104° F] for birds), regardless of the environmental temperature is called warm-bloodedness or homoiothermy (also spelled homeothermy). Warm-blooded animals are able to remain active in situations in which cold-blooded ones cannot. Body temperatures of homoio-therms are kept at a constant value by regulatory mechanisms that counteract the effects of the external environment. In cold envi-ronments, regulatory mechanisms maintain body temperature by increasing heat production and decreasing heat loss. In hot envi-ronments, regulatory mechanisms maintain body temperatures by increasing heat loss. Within a neutral range of several degrees (27°

to 31° C [81° to 88° F] for man), neither heat gain nor heat loss is necessary to maintain body temperature.

Shivering, a regulatory mechanism of many warm-blooded animals, increases heat production. Hibernation, another mechanism used by certain warm-blooded animals, decreases heat loss by means of a general slowing-down of bodily functions. Panting and perspiring are mechanisms for increasing heat loss.

body core, its surrounding muscle layers, the skin-fat layers around them, and the blood. The time constant of the body "compartments" may be quite large. The time constant is the ratio between the thermal capacity of the "compartment" (the heat needed to raise the temperature one degree) and its thermal conductance (the rate at which heat flows into or out of the "compartment"). Larger "compartments" may have a time constant of about an hour. Hence, several hours may pass before a new equilibrium is reached after a sudden change in conditions, such as stepping into the cold from a warm house. This heat stress, or load, is the major disturbance of the thermoregulatory system. The body compensates for it in two ways. In heat conservation, muscles shiver, vasoconstriction (the narrowing of blood vessels) occurs, and cell metabolism increases. In heat dissipation, sweating and vasodilation (the widening of blood vessels) occur. Sweating is the only means by which humans can survive for long in a place where air temperature exceeds body temperature. These reactions are programmed by the brain's hypothalamus from information fed back from its own thermoreceptors and from thermoreceptors in the skin. Thermoregulation has a high set point, about 98° F (37° C), an indication that it is easier for the body to heat itself than to cool itself.

Since some anesthetics can disable the thermoregulatory control centre, patients may need artificial temperature support during surgery. This can be of some advantage because it permits hypothermia, or excessive body cooling. Hypothermia slows body metabolism and is used when heart-lung machines provide oxygen during open-heart surgery. Thermoregulation is not fully developed at birth. That is why adults must protect babies against sharp variations in heat and cold.

Hibernating animals adjust their thermoregulatory systems by lowering the set point to a level just above freezing. Thus they go into a deep torpor. Hibernation reduces the basal metabolic demand so greatly that the animals, if they have stored enough body fat, can survive a severe winter with little or no food. However, the recovery to active conditions is very slow because of the thermal time constants involved.

Thermoregulation and other forms of homeostasis do not maintain a condition at an unvarying level, but within an acceptable range. For example, most people experience a significant daily temperature variation during which body temperature dips nearly two degrees Fahrenheit (one degree Celsius) from an early evening peak to an early morning low.

THE EVOLUTION OF BIOLOGICAL CONTROL SYSTEMS

In the error-activated, negative-feedback control systems that have been described thus far, the mismatch between desired and actual performance keeps errors

Hibernation is a state of greatly reduced metabolic activity and lowered body temperature that certain mammals use to survive adverse winter conditions.

within tolerable limits. However, in the course of evolution, biological control systems employing other strategies for reducing error have developed.

Any well-functioning control system must incorporate stability. For example, if a car hits a bump and suddenly veers, its driver must correct the error quickly but stably. An overcorrection would cause the car to veer in the opposite direction. A basic problem in the design of control systems is the increasingly unstable response that comes about when performance is increased. However, evolutionary processes have selected the biological control systems that operate with satisfactory combinations of speed and stability to perform their required tasks.

Since all complex biological control systems are thought to have evolved from simpler ones, the more complex systems probably developed because the benefits of complexity outweighed the costs, or additional energy, needed to provide it. Whatever system required the least amount of additional energy to yield a given gain would probably have been the one to survive. Thus, the pattern in which blood vessels branch from a single aorta at the heart into about a billion tiny capillaries probably requires less energy to perform its functions than would be needed by any other system. Similarly, at a more conscious level of coordination, a person taking a leisurely walk automatically chooses the combination of pace length and pace frequency that will minimize energy consumption.

VISUAL TRACKING—A CONTROL SYSTEM AT WORK

The analysis of eye movements reveals that the eyes move as a locked pair to maintain stereoscopic, or binocular, vision as they reposition to view new objects. During each saccade, or rapid movement, vision is largely blanked out. Since saccadic movements are very rapid, this blind time is quite brief. A typical saccadic sweep, about ten degrees, is completed in about 50 milliseconds (50/1,000 second), a speed of about 600 degrees per second. (Ten degrees is 1/36 of a complete circle.) The next saccade begins after an interval of about 200 milliseconds. The time between saccades is probably used to evaluate the visual target.

Analysts often make diagrams of the information flow that regulates saccadic eye movements. In such a diagram, the error in eye position is the extent to which the target image is off the fovea, the part of the retina where the best vision occurs. This extent is encoded in light-sensitive cells in the retina and then transmitted through the optic nerve to the brain. The brain area controlling eye movements thereupon issues commands for a correction of eye position. These commands are transmitted to the eye muscles by the oculomotor nerves. The appropriate muscles then contract and move the eyes to give them the best possible view of the target image. Through feedback regulation, this control system should have lessened

Information Flow in Eye Movement Control

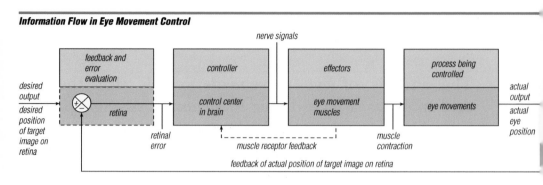

Eye movements are directed by a biological control system. The visual tracking system has a stabilizing mechanism that keeps the eyes on target as the head is repeatedly spun, as during skating, or jarred, as during walking.

the original retinal error. However, the system continues to monitor for inadequacies in the corrective measures taken and for new errors. In addition, the eye muscles contain built-in measuring instruments, called proprioceptors, that feed information back to the brain.

A second mode of eye movement, called smooth tracking, enables eyes to follow a moving target, such as a running animal, a flying bird, a bouncing ball, or a moving train. Unlike saccadic movements, smooth tracking usually keeps the eyes constantly on target without blanking out vision. However, its sweep is only about 30 degrees, or 112 of a complete circle, per second.

The visual tracking system has a stabilizing subsystem that keeps the eyes on target as the head is repeatedly jarred in such activities as walking and running. The stabilization system works through three semicircular canals in each inner ear. These are exquisitely designed small-bore tubes in which fluid moves whenever the head moves. The movements of the fluid trigger nerve signals to the eye movement control system. When the head is jarred in one direction, the canal signals prompt the eyes to move in the opposite direction, keeping the eyes on target. Visual tracking does this too, but the canals' response is faster.

ARTIFICIAL CONTROL SYSTEMS

One of the concerns of bioengineering is to ensure that biological control systems are operating properly. In order to understand and diagnose body functions, it is necessary to use measuring devices that are very sensitive but at the same time have little or no effect upon the body. Faced with this challenge, bioengineers have refined nondestructive testing techniques that had been regarded as too specialized and expensive for industrial application. These nondestructive techniques include tests that use electrical potential and electrical impedance. Electrical potential and impedance are conditions of an electric circuit.

Transducers, devices that convert one form of energy into another form, are used in these systems. The electrical potentials generated by living things are used to measure a variety of biological activities.

Electrical potentials are generated by the heart during the cardiac cycle, by skeletal muscles during contraction, and by nerve cells during voluntary and involuntary actions. The magnitude of such potentials is no more than a few millivolts, and the frequency range does not exceed 200 hertz (cycles per second). Since the impedance of a single neuron may approach 50 to 100 megohms (a megohm is one million ohms), amplifiers with extremely high input impedances have been built for the accurate measurement of these small potentials. (Impedance is a measure of any opposition to the flow of electric current.) When an outside stimulus, or signal, is received by the sensory system, its information is usually transmitted through the organism as an electrical potential. The measurement of these potentials identifies the type of stimulus received and gauges the efficiency of the sensory system. Impedance measurements are a useful way of determining biological properties. The ratio between the mass of body fluids and the mass of surrounding tissue affects the electrical impedance of an organism and its structures. The impedance of body tissues decreases markedly when they are perfused, or soaked, by body fluids. Special instruments can detect the change in impedance and indicate the degree of tissue perfusion. New biosensors are being developed by biomedical engineers. These devices use a biological sensing element, such as enzymes or cells, and are used for laboratory diagnostics and monitoring of living organisms.

MONITORING AND TESTING

Bioengineers have devised patient-monitoring systems that measure, record, and evaluate the four vital functions of health: temperature, respiratory rate, electrical activity of the heart, and blood pressure. Systems can also monitor body fluid composition, fluid balance as indicated by kidney output, and the blood-flow efficiency of the cardiovascular system. Electrical monitoring systems are used most widely to monitor unstable newborn infants and seriously ill, hospitalized patients with heart and respiratory disease. These systems analyze the patterns of signals taken from electrocardiograms, machines that record the electrical output of the heart, and relay the information to the hospital staff, usually as a visual display on an oscilloscope. Any variation in heart rate, blood pressure, or respiratory rate will set off an alarm at the main nursing station of a particular floor or service. Computer-controlled monitoring systems are programmed to analyze the electrocardiogram signal. Whenever the signal becomes abnormal, an alarm alerts the hospital staff. Computers have also been programmed to take a continuous, automatic measurement of the patient's temperature and blood pressure. In addition, computers may store the results of clinical tests, such as blood and urine analyses. Continuous surveillance is the fundamental advantage of computerized patient monitoring.

17

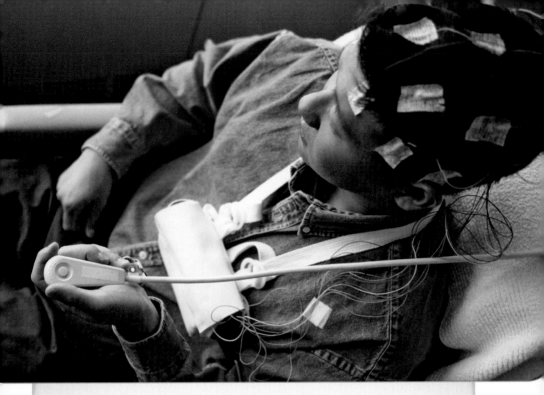

Epilepsy monitoring during a neurological evaluation. Electroencephalogram monitoring can detect abnormalities in the electrical activity of the brain that cause epilepsy.

Computers, in addition, can store and retrieve data comprising the medical records of patients. The medical history of a patient is first stored in a computer database. Selected information can be viewed directly on a monitor or it can be printed out. In some devices, the physician can use a light pen or a mouse for more direct communication with the computer. Expert computerized systems are rapidly being developed by biomedical engineers to provide physicians with possible diagnoses of disease when enough information is fed into the computer. This field, also known as knowledge engineering, or expert systems, involves computer-assisted problem solving. Basically, a computer program sorts through data and applies elements of human expertise or skills in a particular medical field to make a reasonably well-informed diagnosis. Some computerized systems can even assist a physician by advising what kind and how much of a drug should be administered to a critically ill patient. Computers are also programmed to plan certain types of radiation therapy needed for cancer patients.

Some organs, such as the heart, may appear normal at rest but may actually show considerable disease when working at maximum capacity. Stress testing is often used to push the organ to its limits in order to detect problems. One common stress test is done by asking the patient to walk on a treadmill moving at a pre-set speed and uphill angle. While the patient is walking, the heartbeat is observed with an electrocardiogram to detect abnormalities. Other tests involve introducing radioactive compounds, such as thallium, into the body. Subsequent scans of regions in the heart where thallium is present indicate normal tissue, while regions without the element suggest areas of possible damage.

TREATMENT TECHNIQUES

Bioengineers are continuing to develop new techniques for the treatment or correction of disease. For cardiovascular disease, which remains one of the leading causes of death in the United States, traditional methods involve the surgical use of a natural vein graft from the patient to bypass regions of arterial blockage, most often the coronary arteries of the heart. When adequate veins are not available, grafts made from artificial materials such as Dacron and other polymers are substituted. Ongoing studies are attempting to reduce the body's rejection of artificial grafts by coating the artificial materials with the body's own cells prior to implantation—a procedure called endothelial cell seeding.

Newer devices have been developed that provide less traumatic, simpler, and less expensive means of treatment. Balloon angioplasty procedures involve inserting a catheter, or thin tube, with a deflated balloon attached to its tip into an artery to break apart arterial obstructions. Once in place, the balloon is inflated against the obstruction until it compresses the plaque into the artery wall. This opens up the inside of the artery and increases the blood flow through the artery. Modifications to this approach include catheter-tip lasers, which ablate, or vaporize, the plaque, and atherectomy devices, which use a sharp, rotating blade to cut the plaque from the vessel wall.

Lasers can also be found in surgical procedures in which their clean and precise cutting ability is used to open tissues. In other devices, their high heat-generating capacity is used to weld tissues together. This is a preferred technique for retinal repair. Photodynamic therapy against solid cancerous tumours begins by incorporating into the body a special dye that attaches only to the tumour. An argon ion laser then activates the dye and destroys the tumour using the intense heat the laser generates.

Ultrasonic energy—energy at low frequencies and very high power levels—can be used to disintegrate abnormal tissues in a procedure called ultrasonic lithotripsy. With this procedure, physicians can relieve patients suffering from painful kidney stones by selectively focusing powerful ultrasound waves at the stones. As this energy hits the hardened stones, it can break the stones into small fragments that are then more easily eliminated through the urinary system.

Functional electrical stimulation (FES) is a procedure used to restore control of denervated muscles, individual muscles that have become paralyzed, often by injury. These muscles can be stimulated by electrical signals applied under computer control. These signals then produce a contraction. Stimulating multiple muscle groups in sequence can provide restoration of some body motion, such as arm movement or even walking.

Drug delivery systems are devices implanted within the body that use a computer to control the amount of drug administered to a patient on a regular basis. Infusion pumps provide drugs directly to the bloodstream. This procedure is sometimes performed using insulin for diabetics, antihypertensive drugs to fight high blood pressure, and various chemotherapeutic drugs and anesthetics for cancer patients.

CHAPTER 2

DIAGNOSTIC IMAGING

The ability to "see" inside the body is very important for accurate diagnosis. Endoscopes are tubes with many fiberglass bundles that both transmit and collect light. These devices are inserted into the body through natural openings or incisions and provide pictures of tissues. Ultrasound is sound energy at frequencies above the level of normal human hearing (that is, above 20,000 hertz). Like X-rays, ultrasound can present an image of body structures. Unlike X-rays, however, well-controlled ultrasound is harmless to tissue, and can be used repeatedly over a long time period. Biological measurement with ultrasound is possible because its propagation, or transmission, varies with the mechanical properties of the tissue. Because various tissues absorb and scatter ultrasonic energy differently, ultrasound is often used for the detection of boundaries between various types of tissue, such as that between skin and muscle. Standard two-dimensional and prototype three-dimensional ultrasonic imaging can also detect changes in organs due to disease. Such changes include the build-up of athero-sclerotic plaques in arteries or the development of tumours in the liver and other organs. Very high fre-quency ultrasound transducers are also mounted on the tips of catheters that can be inserted into specific blood vessels to obtain images of the insides of arteries. Fur-thermore, the constant motion of blood cells changes the frequency with which ultrasound is reflected off of them. Thus, bioengineers can determine the speed of blood flow in any part of the body by measuring the frequency of reflected ultrasonic waves and converting this into colour-coded flow images.

In addition to standard X-ray devices, computed X-ray tomography (CT) scanners can provide greater detail using advanced radiographic techniques. Using multiple X-ray sources and detectors arranged in a hollow ring, high-resolution images can be obtained of the body in cross section. By combining several cross-sectional images along the body's long axis (the line from head to foot), three-dimensional images can be generated. Nuclear medicine procedures allow selective imaging of body regions that have absorbed specialized radioactive materials. By scanning over these regions with gamma-ray detectors, it is possible to generate an image based on the uptake or metabolism of certain "tagged" compounds, such as barium. A newer technique involves the production of images using the magnetic properties of various elements. The element hydrogen, which is contained in all organic molecules, can be monitored with magnetic resonance imaging (MRI). The procedure begins by inserting the body into a large magnet. This causes the magnetic spin of the hydrogen nuclei to align with the magnet. Radiofrequency signals are then used to alter that spin alignment temporarily, producing a distinctive magnetic echo when the signal is discontinued. Emitted echoes from throughout the body can then be used to make images of certain organs based upon the hydrogen concentration of each organ. Positron-emission tomography (PET) and single-photon-emission tomography (SPECT) utilize the release of high-energy gamma rays from radioactive particles transmitted through the body to form an image based on the location of the emitting source.

X-RAYS

Used since 1895, X-rays were the first type of radiation to provide images of the interior of the body. X-rays pass through bodily tissues and also have the property of darkening photographic film when they strike it. As they penetrate tissues, the X rays are absorbed differentially, with denser objects such as bones absorbing more of the rays and thus preventing them from reaching the film. Soft tissues, on the other hand, absorb fewer rays; the result is that in an X-ray photograph of the interior of the body, bones show up as lighter areas and soft tissues show up as darker ones on the exposed film.

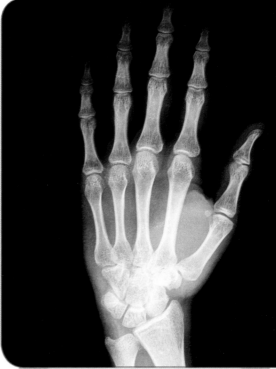

If a photographic plate that is sensitive to X-rays is placed behind a part of the body and an X-ray source is placed in front, X-ray exposure will result in a picture of the internal bones and organs.

A limiting factor in X-rays when used alone is the inability to distinguish between adjacent, differentiated soft tissues of roughly the same density (i.e., it is not possible to produce contrasting tones between such objects on the exposed film). To obtain this contrast, a contrast medium—a liquid or gaseous substance that is comparatively opaque to X-rays (radiopaque) or comparatively transparent to them—is injected into the body. Contrast-medium fluids can be injected into naturally occurring body cavities, injected into the bloodstream and lymphatic vessels, swallowed or introduced by enema for study of the digestive tract, or injected around organs to show their external contour. Different contrast media thus allow the X-ray imaging of particular types of soft internal structures, such as the arteries and veins in angiography, the passage of blood through the heart in angiocardiography, the gallbladder and biliary channels in cholecystography, the spinal cord in myelography, and the urinary tract in urography. Virtually any part of the body can be examined for physiological disturbances of the normal structures by X-ray analysis. X-ray motion-picture films can record the body processes as the contrast media enter and leave parts of the body.

NUCLEAR MEDICINE

Nuclear medicine, the medical specialty that involves the use of radioactive isotopes in the diagnosis and treatment of disease, began only after the discovery by Enrico Fermi in 1935 that stable elements could be made radioactive by bombarding them with neutrons. The atoms of the elements so bombarded capture these neutrons, thus assuming a different nuclear form while remaining the same elements. These radioisotopes have unstable nuclei, however, and dissipate excess energy by emitting radiation in the form of gamma and other rays.

In isotope scanning, a radioisotope is introduced into the body, usually by means of intravenous injection. The isotope is then taken up in different amounts by different organs. Its distribution can be determined by recording the radiation it emits, and through charting its concentration it is often possible to recognize the presence, size, and shape of various abnormalities in body organs. The radiation emitted is detected by a scintillation counter, which is moved back and forth over the organ being scanned; these messages can then be electronically recorded and studied by clinicians. The radioisotope usually has a short half-life and thus decays completely before its radioactivity can cause any damage to the patient's body.

Different isotopes tend to concentrate in particular organs: for example, iodine-131 settles in the thyroid gland and can reveal a variety of defects in thyroid functioning. Another isotope, carbon-14, is useful in studying abnormalities of metabolism that underlie diabetes, gout, anemia, and acromegaly. Various scanning devices and techniques have been developed, including tomography and magnetic resonance imaging.

One of the most-used nuclear medicine techniques in diagnosis and biomedical research is positron emission tomography (PET). It has proven particularly useful for studying brain and heart functions and certain biochemical processes involving these organs (e.g., glucose metabolism and oxygen

BRAIN SCANNING

Both isotope scanning and X-ray photography are used in brain scanning, or the use of diagnostic methods for detecting intracranial abnormalities. The oldest of the brain-scanning procedures still in use is a simple, relatively non-invasive procedure called isotope scanning. It is based on the tendency of certain radioactive isotopes to concentrate selectively in tumours and blood vessel lesions. The procedure involves the injection of a radioactive isotope (such as technetium-99m or iodine-131) into a blood vessel that supplies the cranial region. As the substance becomes localized within the brain, it decays, therewith emitting gamma rays. The concentration of rays at a given site, as measured by a movable radiation detection device, can reveal the presence, the shape, and often the size of the intracranial abnormality. In many cases, isotope scanning has been replaced by computerized axial tomography (CAT), or computed tomography (CT).

The CAT scan is a procedure in which the brain is X-rayed from many different angles. An X-ray source delivers a series of short pulses of radiation as it and an electronic detector are rotated around the head of the individual being tested. The responses of the detector are fed to a computer that analyzes and integrates the X-ray data from the numerous scans to construct a detailed cross-sectional image of the brain. A series of such images enables physicians to locate brain tumours, cerebral abscesses, blood clots, and other disorders that would be difficult to detect with conventional X-ray techniques.

With the development in the mid-1970s of the CAT scan, computer-based technologies have revolutionized the field of medical diagnosis. One of the more significant tomographic techniques is nuclear magnetic resonance (NMR) imaging. Like CAT, NMR generates images of thin slices of the brain (or other organ under study), but it does so without the hazard of X-rays or other ionizing radiation. In addition NMR can reveal physiological and biochemical, as well as structural, abnormalities. (Although the benefits of NMR are myriad, the technique is not advised for individuals with pacemakers, aneurysm clips, large metallic prostheses, or dependence on iron-containing instruments.) Positron emission tomography (PET) is a computer-based procedure in which a radioactive tracer-labeled compound is introduced into the brain (or other organ under study), and its behaviour is tracked. This information, with computer modeling, eventually yields a cross-sectional image of the physiological process under study.

uptake). In PET a chemical compound labeled with a short-lived positron-emitting radionuclide of carbon, oxygen, nitrogen, or fluorine is injected into the body. The activity of such a radiopharmaceutical is quantitatively measured throughout the target organs by means of photomultiplier-scintillator detectors. As the radionuclide decays, positrons are annihilated by electrons, giving rise to gamma rays that are detected simultaneously by the photomultiplier-scintillator combinations positioned on opposite sides of the patient. The data from the detectors are analyzed, integrated, and reconstructed by means of a computer to produce images of the organs being scanned.

PET has become a valuable tool in the detection of cancer and cancer metastasis (spread) and in the evaluation of heart conditions. PET studies have helped scientists understand more about how drugs affect the brain and what happens during learning, when using language, and in certain brain disorders, such as stroke, depression, and Parkinson disease. In addition, scientists are working to find ways to use PET to identify the biochemical nature of neurological disorders and mental disorders and to determine how well therapy is working in patients. PET has revealed marked changes in the depressed brain, and knowing the location of these changes helps researchers understand the causes of depression and monitor the effectiveness of specific treatments.

MAGNETIC RESONANCE IMAGING

Magnetic resonance imaging is a three-dimensional diagnostic imaging technique used to visualize organs and structures inside the body without the need for X-rays or other radiation. MRI is valuable for providing detailed anatomical images and can reveal minute changes that occur over time. It can be used to detect structural abnormalities that appear in the course of a disease as well as how these abnormalities affect subsequent development and how their progression corelates with mental and emotional aspects of a disorder. Since MRI poorly visualizes bone, excellent images of the intracranial and intraspinal contents are produced.

During an MRI procedure, the patient lies inside a massive hollow cylindrical magnet and is exposed to a powerful steady magnetic field. Different atoms in the portion of the body being scanned resonate to different frequencies of magnetic fields. MRI is used primarily to detect the oscillations of hydrogen atoms, which contain a proton nucleus that spins and thus can be thought of as possessing a small magnetic field. In MRI a background magnetic field lines up all the hydrogen atoms in the tissue being imaged. A second magnetic field, oriented differently from the background field, is turned on and off many times per second; at certain pulse rates, the hydrogen atoms resonate and line up with this second field. When the second field is turned off, the atoms that were lined up with it swing back to align with the background field. As they swing back, they create a signal that can be picked up and converted into an image.

Tissue that contains a large amount of hydrogen, which occurs abundantly in the human body in the form of water, produces a bright image, whereas tissue that contains little or no hydrogen (e.g., bone) appears black. The brightness of an MRI image is facilitated by the use of a contrast agent such as gadodiamide, which patients ingest or are injected with prior to the procedure.

Although these agents can improve the quality of images from MRI, the procedure remains relatively limited in its sensitivity. Techniques to improve the sensitivity of MRI are being developed. The most promising of these techniques involves the use of para-hydrogen, a form of hydrogen with unique molecular spin properties that are highly sensitive to magnetic fields.

Refinement of the magnetic fields used in MRI has led to the development of highly sensitive imaging

MRI scans generally last for between 15 and 90 minutes. Patients must remain very still during scans. Though patients rarely feel anything during the procedure, the machine is very loud.

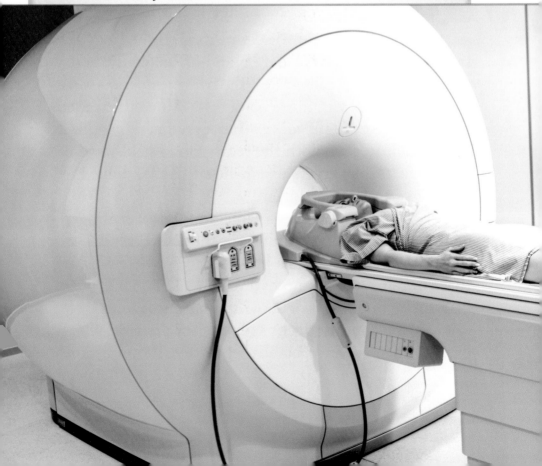

techniques, such as diffusion MRI and functional MRI, that are designed to image very specific properties of tissues. In addition, magnetic resonance angiography, a unique form of MRI technology, can be used to produce an image of flowing blood. This permits the visualization of arteries and veins without the need for needles, catheters, or contrast agents. As with MRI, these techniques have helped revolutionize biomedical research and diagnosis.

Advanced computer technologies have made it possible for radiologists to construct holograms that provide three-dimensional images from the digital cross sections obtained by conventional MRI scanners. These holograms can be useful in locating lesions precisely. MRI is particularly valuable in imaging the brain, the spinal cord, pelvic organs such as the urinary bladder, and cancellous (or spongy) bone. It reveals the precise extent of tumours rapidly and vividly, and it provides early evidence of potential damage from stroke, allowing physicians to administer proper treatments early. MRI also has largely supplanted arthrography, the injection of dye into a joint to visualize cartilage or ligament damage, and myelography,

the injection of dye into the spinal canal to visualize spinal cord or intervertebral disk abnormalities.

Because patients must lie quietly inside a narrow tube, MRI may raise anxiety levels in patients, especially those with claustrophobia. Another disadvantage of MRI is that it has a longer scanning time than some other imaging tools, including computerized axial tomography (CAT). This makes MRI sensitive to motion artifacts and thus of less value in scanning the chest or abdomen. Because of the strong magnetic field, MRI cannot be used if a pacemaker is present or if metal is present in critical areas such as the eye or the brain.

ULTRASONICS

The term "ultrasonics" refers to vibrations of frequencies greater than the upper limit of the audible range for humans—that is, greater than about 20 kilohertz. The term "sonic" is applied to ultrasound waves of very high amplitudes. Hypersound, sometimes called praetersound or microsound, is sound waves of frequencies greater than 10^{13} hertz. At such high frequencies it is very difficult for a sound wave to propagate efficiently; indeed, above a frequency of about 1.25×10^{13} hertz it is impossible for longitudinal waves to propagate at all, even in a liquid or a solid, because the molecules of the material in which the waves are traveling cannot pass the vibration along rapidly enough.

Many animals have the ability to hear sounds in the human ultrasonic frequency range. A presumed sensitivity of roaches and rodents to frequencies in the 40 kilohertz region has led to the manufacture of "pest controllers" that emit loud sounds in that frequency range to drive the pests away, but they do not appear to work as advertised.

TRANSDUCERS

An ultrasonic transducer is a device used to convert some other type of energy into an ultrasonic vibration. There are several basic types, classified by the energy source and by the medium into which the waves are being generated. Mechanical devices include gas-driven, or pneumatic, transducers such as whistles as well as liquid-driven transducers such as hydrodynamic oscillators and vibrating blades. These devices, limited to low ultrasonic frequencies, have a number of industrial applications, including drying, ultrasonic cleaning, and injection of fuel oil into burners. Electromechanical transducers are far more versatile and include piezoelectric and magnetostrictive devices. A magnetostrictive transducer makes use of a type of magnetic material in which an applied oscillating magnetic field squeezes the atoms of the material together, creating a periodic change in the length of the material and thus producing a high-frequency mechanical vibration. Magnetostrictive transducers are used primarily in the lower frequency ranges and are common in ultrasonic cleaners and ultrasonic machining applications.

By far the most popular and versatile type of ultrasonic transducer is the piezoelectric crystal, which converts an oscillating electric field applied to the crystal into a mechanical vibration. Piezoelectric crystals include quartz, Rochelle salt, and certain types of ceramic. Piezoelectric transducers are readily employed over the entire frequency range and at all output levels. Particular shapes can be chosen for particular applications. For example, a disc shape provides a plane ultrasonic wave, while curving the radiating surface in a slightly concave or bowl shape creates an ultrasonic wave that will focus at a specific point.

Piezoelectric and magnetostrictive transducers also are employed as ultrasonic receivers, picking up an ultrasonic vibration and converting it into an electrical oscillation.

MEDICAL APPLICATIONS

Although ultrasound competes with other forms of medical imaging, such as X-ray techniques and magnetic resonance imaging, it has certain desirable features—for example, Doppler motion study—that the other techniques cannot provide. In addition, among the various modern techniques for the imaging of internal organs, ultrasonic devices are by far the least expensive.

Ultrasound is also used for treating joint pains and for treating certain types of tumours for which it is desirable to produce localized heating. A very effective use of ultrasound deriving from its nature as a mechanical vibration is the elimination of kidney and bladder stones.

Much medical diagnostic imaging is carried out with X-rays. Because of the high photon energies of the X-ray, this type of radiation is highly ionizing—that is, X-rays are readily capable of destroying molecular bonds in the body tissue through which they pass. This destruction can lead to changes in the function of the tissue involved or, in extreme cases, its annihilation.

One of the important advantages of ultrasound is that it is a mechanical vibration and is therefore a nonionizing form of energy. Thus, it is usable in many sensitive circumstances where X-rays might be damaging. Also, the resolution of X-rays is limited owing to their great penetrating ability and the slight differences between soft tissues. Ultrasound, on the other hand, gives good contrast between various types of soft tissue.

Ultrasonic scanning in medical diagnosis uses the same principle as sonar. Pulses of high-frequency ultrasound, generally above one megahertz, are created by a piezoelectric transducer and directed into the body. As the ultrasound traverses various internal organs, it encounters changes in acoustic impedance, which cause reflections. The amount and time delay of the various reflections can be analyzed to obtain

information regarding the internal organs. In the B-scan mode, a linear array of transducers is used to scan a plane in the body, and the resultant data is displayed on a television screen as a two-dimensional plot. The A-scan technique uses a single transducer to scan along a line in the body, and the echoes are plotted as a function of time. This technique is used for measuring the distances or sizes of internal organs. The M-scan mode is used to record the motion of internal organs, as in the study of heart dysfunction. Greater resolution is obtained in ultrasonic imaging by using higher frequencies—i.e., shorter wavelengths. A limitation of this property of waves is that higher frequencies tend to be much more strongly absorbed.

Because it is nonionizing, ultrasound has become one of the staples of obstetric diagnosis. During the process of drawing amniotic fluid in testing for birth defects, ultrasonic imaging is used to guide the needle and thus avoid damage to the fetus or surrounding tissue. Ultrasonic imaging of the fetus can be used to determine the date of conception, to identify multiple births, and to diagnose abnormalities in the development of the fetus.

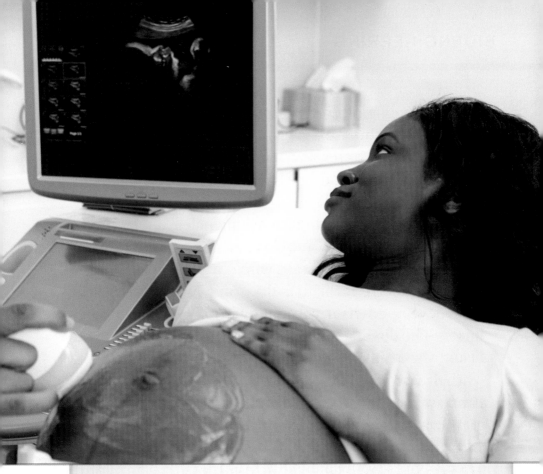

This pregnant woman is getting a 4D ultrasound, which produces moving 3D images. Ultrasounds in 4D are made up of sections of several real-time 2D images.

Ultrasonic Doppler techniques have become very important in diagnosing problems in blood flow. In one technique, a three-megahertz ultrasonic beam is reflected off typical oncoming arterial blood with a Doppler shift of a few kilohertz—a frequency difference that can be heard directly by a physician. Using this technique, it is possible to monitor the heartbeat of a fetus long before a stethoscope can pick up the sound. Arterial diseases such as arteriosclerosis can also be diagnosed, and the healing of arteries can be monitored following surgery. A combination of B-scan imaging and Doppler imaging, known as duplex scanning, can identify arteries and immediately measure their blood flow; this has been extensively used to diagnose heart valve defects.

Using ultrasound with frequencies up to 2,000 megahertz, which has a wavelength of 0.75 micrometre in soft tissues (as compared with a wavelength of about 0.55 micrometre for light), ultrasonic microscopes have been developed that rival light microscopes in their resolution. The distinct advantage of ultrasonic microscopes lies in their ability to distinguish various parts of a cell by their viscosity. Also, because they require no artificial contrast mediums, which kill the cells, acoustic microscopy can study actual living cells.

DIAGNOSTIC GRAPHING TECHNIQUES

Not all useful diagnostic techniques produce images of body parts. Some techniques, such as electrocardiography and electroencephalography, yield graphs that illustrate the electrical activity in a particular part of the body.

ELECTROCARDIOGRAPHY

Electrocardiography is a method of graphic tracing that produces an electrocardiogram (ECG or EKG) of the electric current generated by the heart muscle during a heartbeat. The tracing is recorded with an electrocardiograph (actually a relatively simple string galvanometer), and it provides information on the condition and performance of the heart. The Dutch physiologist Willem Einthoven developed the first electrocardiogram in 1903, and for many years the tracing was called an EKG after the German "Elektrokardiogramm." During the late 1960s, computerized electrocardiography came into use in many of the larger hospitals.

Electrocardiograms are made by applying electrodes to various parts of the body. Electrodes that record the electrical activity of the heart are placed at 10 different locations: one on each of the four limbs and six at different locations on the anterior surface of the chest. After the electrodes are in place, held with a salt paste, a millivolt from a source outside the body is introduced so that the instrument can be calibrated. Standardizing electrocardiograms makes it possible to compare them as taken from person to person and from time to time from the same person.

The normal electrocardiogram shows typical upward and downward deflections that reflect the alternate contraction of the atria (the two upper chambers) and of the ventricles (the two lower chambers) of the heart. The first upward deflection, P, is due to atrial contraction and is known as the atrial complex. The other deflections—Q, R, S, and T—are all due to the action

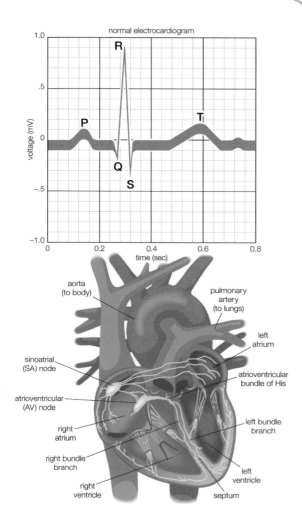

normal electrocardiogram

of the ventricles and are known as the ventricular complexes. Any deviation from the norm in a particular electrocardiogram is indicative of a possible heart disorder.

The electrocardiogram is of greatest use in diagnosing cardiac arrhythmias, acute and prior myocardial infarctions (heart attacks), pericardial disease, and cardiac enlargement (atrial and ventricular). The presence of hypertension (high blood pressure), thyroid disease, and certain types of malnutrition also may be revealed by an electrocardiogram.

On top, an electrocardiogram shows the deflections that reflect the alternate contractions of the atria and ventricles during a heartbeat. At the bottom is a diagram of the heart.

In addition, electrocardiography can be used to determine whether a slow heart rate is physiological or is caused by heart block. The exercise electrocardiogram, or ECG stress test, is used to assess the ability of the coronary arteries to deliver oxygen while the heart is undergoing strain imposed by a standardized exercise protocol. If the blood supply to the heart is jeopardized during exercise, the inadequate oxygenation of the heart muscle is recorded by typical changes in the electrocardiogram that indicate coronary heart disease (narrowing of the coronary arteries). However, a normal electrocardiogram does not exclude significant coronary heart disease and is not predictive of disease course.

ELECTROENCEPHALOGRAPHY

The aim of electroencephalography is to record the electrical activity of the brain. The nerve cells of the brain generate electrical impulses that fluctuate rhythmically in distinct patterns. In 1929 German scientist Hans Berger developed an electroencephalograph, an instrument that measures and records these brain-wave patterns. The recording produced by such an instrument is called an electroencephalogram, commonly abbreviated EEG.

To record the electrical activity of the brain, 8 to 16 pairs of electrodes are attached to the scalp. Each pair of electrodes transmits a signal to one of several recording channels of the electroencephalograph. This signal consists of the difference in the voltage between the pair. The rhythmic fluctuation of this potential difference is shown as peaks and troughs on a line graph by the recording channel. The EEG of a normal adult in a fully conscious but relaxed state is made up of regularly recurring oscillating waves known as alpha waves. When a person is excited or startled, the alpha waves are replaced by low-voltage, rapid, irregular waves. During sleep, the brain waves become extremely slow. Such is also the case when a person is in a deep coma. Other abnormal conditions are associated with

This patient is demonstrating normal cerebral activity according to the electroencephalogram (EEG) displayed on the screen next to her.

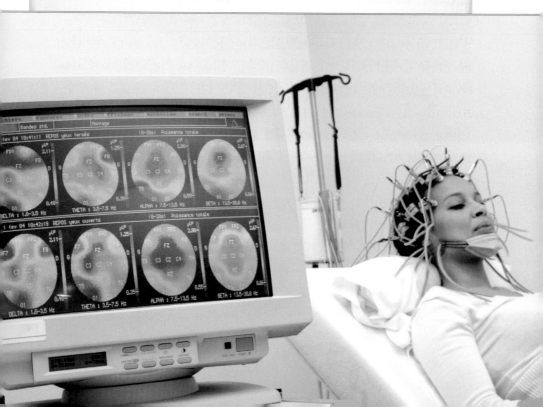

particular EEG patterns. For example, irregular slow waves known as delta waves arise from the vicinity of a localized area of brain damage.

Electroencephalography provides a means of studying how the brain works and of tracing connections between one part of the central nervous system and another. However, its effectiveness as a research tool is limited because it records only a small sample of electrical activity from the surface of the brain. Many of the more complex functions of the brain, such as those that underlie emotions and thought, cannot be related closely to EEG patterns. Furthermore, the EEG is of no use in diagnosing psychiatric illness.

Electroencephalography has proved more useful as a diagnostic aid in cases of serious head injuries, brain tumours, cerebral infections, sleep disorders, epilepsy, and various degenerative diseases of the nervous system. Electroencephalography is also useful in the assessment of patients with suspected brain death. This is particularly important if organs are to be saved for transplantation as soon as brain death has been confirmed. Sleep deprivation and other provocative tests, including photic (light) stimulation and hyperventilation, can be used to accentuate borderline findings.

CHAPTER 3

PROSTHESES

T he design of prosthetic devices, or prostheses, to replace missing or malfunctioning body parts was one of the earliest branches of biomedical engineering to be developed. Prosthetic devices now in use range from artificial limbs used to replace diseased, missing, or malfunctioning limbs to systems that duplicate the function of critical body organs.

The artificial parts that are most commonly thought of as prostheses are those that replace lost arms and legs, but bone, artery, and heart valve replacements are common, and artificial eyes and teeth are also correctly termed prostheses. The term is sometimes extended to cover such things as eyeglasses and hearing aids, which improve the functioning of a part. The medical specialty that deals with prostheses is called prosthetics. The origin of prosthetics as a science is attributed to the 16th-century French surgeon Ambroise Paré. Later workers developed upper-extremity replacements, including metal hands made either in one piece or with movable parts. The solid metal hand of the 16th and 17th centuries later gave way in great measure to a single hook or a leather-covered, nonfunctioning hand attached to the forearm by a leather or wooden shell. Improvement in the design of prostheses and increased acceptance of their use have accompanied major wars. New lightweight materials and better mechanical joints were introduced after World Wars I and II.

PROSTHETIC LIMBS AND JOINTS

One type of below-knee prosthesis is made from plastic and fits the below-knee stump with total contact. It is held on either by means of a strap that passes above the kneecap or by means of rigid metal knee hinges attached to a leather thigh corset. Weight bearing is accomplished by pressure of the prosthesis against the tendon that extends from the kneecap to the lower legbone. In addition, a foot piece is commonly used that consists of a solid foot and ankle with layers of rubber in the heel to give a cushioning effect.

There are two main types of above-knee prostheses: (1) the prosthesis held on by means of a belt around the pelvis or suspended from the shoulder by straps and (2) the prosthesis kept in contact with the leg stump by suction, the belt and shoulder straps being eliminated.

The more complicated prosthesis used in cases of amputation through the hip joint or half of the pelvis usually consists of a plastic socket, in which the person virtually sits; a mechanical hip joint of metal; and a leather, plastic, or wooden thigh piece with the mechanical knee, shin portion, and foot as described above.

A great advance in fabrication of functional upper-extremity prostheses followed World War II. Arm prostheses came to be made of plastic, frequently reinforced with glass fibres.

The below-elbow prosthesis consists of a single plastic shell and a metal wrist joint to which is attached a terminal device, either a hook or a hand. The person wears a shoulder harness made of webbing, from which a steel cable extends to the terminal device. When the person shrugs the shoulder, thus tightening the cable, the terminal device opens and closes. In certain cases the biceps muscle may be attached to the prosthesis by a surgical operation known as cineplasty. This procedure makes it possible to dispense with the shoulder harness and allows finer control of the terminal device. The above-elbow prosthesis has, in addition to the forearm shell, an upper-arm plastic shell and a mechanical, locking elbow joint. This complicates its use, inasmuch as there must be one cable control for the terminal device and another control to lock and unlock the elbow. The

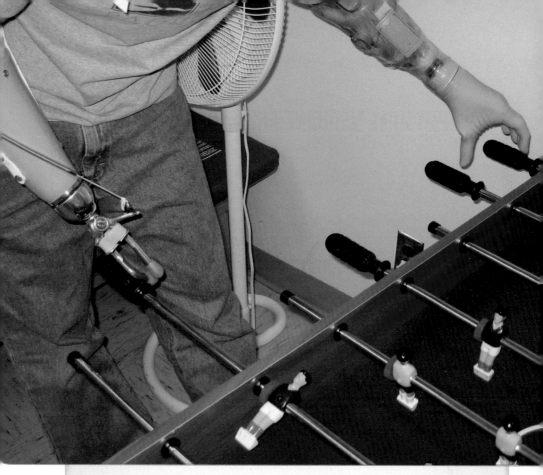

This photo from the Walter Reed Army Medical Center, in Bethesda, Md., shows an American soldier with two prostheses playing table football.

most complicated upper-extremity prosthesis, that used in cases of amputation through the shoulder, includes a plastic shoulder cap extending over the chest and back. Usually no shoulder rotation is possible, but the mechanical elbow and terminal device function as in other arm prostheses.

A metal hook that opens and closes as two fingers is the most commonly used terminal device and the most efficient. After World War II the APRL hand

PHYSICAL MEDICINE AND REHABILITATION

Also called physiatry or rehabilitation medicine, physical medicine and rehabilitation is the medical specialty concerned with the diagnosis, treatment, and prevention of physical impairments, particularly those associated with disorders of the muscles, nerves, bones, or brain. This specialized medical service is generally aimed at rehabilitating persons disabled by pain or ailments affecting the motor functions of the body.

In the late 20th century high technology was increasingly harnessed in efforts to rehabilitate paraplegics, quadriplegics, and others with severely impaired motor functions. Microcomputers were developed that could send precisely coordinated jolts of electricity directly into the muscles of such patients, mimicking the cerebral impulses that could no longer reach their muscle destinations because of a severed spinal cord. The microcomputers' sophisticated programs enable them to contract a patient's muscles in unison so that he can actually stand and sit, walk, and even use his hands to perform relatively fine movements. Such devices were still in the experimental stage and were costly to make and use, but they seemed to be the most promising development yet in efforts to restore the power of movement to nerve injury victims.

Other, less ambitious devices to help paralyzed patients include wheelchairs with specially equipped control systems that can be operated by the mouth and teeth movements of a quadriplegic. Mobile robotic arms have been developed that are equipped with a video camera so that they can move safely and intelligently about a patient's house. These personal robots can receive and execute oral commands from the patient to perform such simple household tasks as filling a glass with water or taking a book off a shelf.

Functional training teaches the impaired individual how to carry out most safely and effectively the activities of daily life. This training may mean learning to use crutches, a brace, or an artificial arm or it may involve working out and practicing the movements required to do housework with the use of only one hand or the way to board public transportation with a stiff leg. Such training often requires long hours of practice; it may be facilitated by use of devices that make it easier to fasten buttons, hold a fork, or dial a telephone.

(from U.S. Army Prosthetic Research Laboratory) was developed. This is a metal mechanical hand covered by a rubber glove of a colour similar to that of the patient's remaining hand. Many attempts have been made to use electrical energy as the source of hook or hand control. This is done primarily by building into the arm prosthesis electrodes that are activated by the patient's own muscle contractions. The electric current generated by these muscle contractions is then amplified by means of electrical components and batteries to control the terminal device. Such an arrangement is referred to as a myoelectrical control system.

Patients unable to walk due to disabling diseases or injuries can often return to normal activities when their hip and knee joints are replaced with artificial joints. Most artificial joints are made from metals such as titanium, which have high strength, low weight, and good compatibility with body tissues. These devices are surgically inserted into the adjacent, healthy bone and fixed in place using an orthopedic bone cement called polymethylmethacrylate, or PMMA. Because metals that rub against other metals eventually wear down and produce hazardous splintered particles that may migrate throughout the body, bioengineers have developed polymers, such as polyethylene, that are less likely to wear down. Metal surfaces are designed to articulate, or move, against these polymer surfaces. Joints that bear little force, such as the fingers, can be made entirely of polymeric materials.

With the advent of computer-aided design (CAD) systems, biomedical engineers and orthopedic surgeons can design and build a prosthesis that is customized to an individual patient. The anatomy of the part to be replaced is recorded by an imaging technique and then transmitted into a CAD system, which then determines an optimal design for that device. Precise digital measurements of the model are sent to a computer-driven milling machine that produces the implant exactly to specifications. Many kinds of artificial arms, for example, have been designed in this way. These arms are often powered by an electric motor or by an air-driven or hydraulic-piston assembly. Simpler artificial arms permit only grasping movements, while other, more sensitive prostheses may also make very fine wrist and elbow movement possible. The number and types of signals needed to operate a prostheses depend on the amount of control required. An artificial arm that moves only up and down requires only two signals. However, if the replacement limb must also be capable of more extensive movements, such as rotatory and grasping motions, many signals are needed. Electromyographic signals, signals generated by muscles, can sometimes be made to control artificial limbs. For effective operation, an electromyographic signal system requires feedback from the limb in order to sense and control movement of the limb. Pressure sensors at the tips of an artificial limb perform this function. Some artificial limbs can be switched on and off by signals sent through eye movements and can be controlled by varying the amount of pressure put on strain-sensitive skin sensors.

THE HEART

An artificial heart is a device that maintains blood circulation and oxygenation in the human body for varying periods of time. The two main types of artificial hearts are the heart-lung machine and the mechanical heart. Along with artificial hearts, biomedical engineers have also developed pacemakers, medical devices that are implanted in patients' hearts to regulate their heartbeats.

THE HEART-LUNG MACHINE

The heart-lung machine is a mechanical pump that maintains a patient's blood circulation and oxygenation during heart surgery by diverting blood from the venous system, directing it through tubing into an artificial lung (oxygenator), and returning it to the body. The oxygenator removes carbon dioxide and adds oxygen to the blood that is pumped into the arterial system. The blood pumped back into the patient's arteries is sufficient to maintain life at even the most distant parts of the body as well as in those organs with the greatest requirements (e.g., brain, kidneys, and liver). To do this, up to 1.3 gallons (5 litres) or more of blood must be pumped each minute. While the heart is relieved of its pumping duties, it can be stopped, and the surgeon can perform open-heart surgery that may include valve repair or replacement, repair of defects inside the heart, or revascularization of blocked arteries.

The first successful clinical use of a heart-lung machine was reported by American surgeon John H. Gibbon, Jr., in 1953. During this operation for the surgical closure of an atrial septal defect, cardiopulmonary bypass was achieved by a machine equipped with an oxygenator developed by Gibbon and a roller pump developed in 1932 by American surgeon Michael E. DeBakey. Since then, heart-lung machines have been greatly improved with smaller and more-efficient oxygenators, allowing them to be used not only in adults but also in children and even newborn infants.

MECHANICAL HEARTS

Mechanical hearts, which include total artificial hearts and ventricular assist devices (VADs), are machines that are capable of replacing or assisting the pumping action of the heart for prolonged periods without causing excessive damage to the blood components. Implantation of a total artificial heart requires removal of both of the patient's ventricles (lower chambers). However, with the use of a VAD to support either the right or the left ventricle, the entire heart remains in the body. Mechanical hearts are implanted only after maximal medical management has failed. They may be used for cardiac resuscitation after cardiac arrest, for recovery from cardiogenic shock after heart surgery, and in some patients with chronic heart failure who are waiting for a heart transplant. Occasionally, mechanical hearts have been used as a permanent support in patients who do not qualify for a heart transplant or as a bridge to recovery of the patient's own diseased heart. The goal is to provide a safe, effective system that allows the recipient to move about freely, thus improving the quality of life. Some recipients of VADs have lived several years and have returned to work and normal physical activities.

A left VAD pumps oxygenated blood from the left ventricle to the aorta. The pumping part of the device is implanted in the left upper abdomen or left side of the chest. A tube from the pump exits the skin and connects to a controller that regulates the function of the pump and to a power source. Pneumatic devices have membranes or sacs that are moved by air pressure to pump the blood, while electrical devices use electro-mechanical systems for power. Electrical devices are being developed that are totally implantable and do not require a tube exiting the skin; with these devices, power to the pump is transmitted between external and internal batteries through the intact skin.

Most mechanical hearts incorporate various centrifugal pumps, paracorporeal pulsatile pumps, cardiopulmonary bypass (CPB) pumps, and the intra-aortic balloon pump (IABP). These pumps generate a pulsatile blood flow and pressure similar to those of the natural heart. Smaller devices known as axial flow pumps, on the other hand, generate continuous blood flow by a jet-engine type of technology. An experienced surgical team chooses the particular device to be implanted by assessing the patient's size, the amount of support the heart requires, and the expected duration of support.

The first successful use of a mechanical heart in a human was performed by Michael E. DeBakey in 1966. After surgery to replace the patient's aorta and mitral valve, a left VAD was installed, making it possible to wean the patient from the heart-lung machine; after 10 days of pump flow from the VAD, the heart recovered, and the VAD was removed. During the 1970s synthetic materials were developed that greatly aided the development of permanent artificial hearts. One such device, designed by American physician Robert K. Jarvik, was surgically implanted into a patient by American surgeon William C. DeVries in 1982. The aluminum and plastic device, called the Jarvik-7 for its inventor, replaced the patient's two ventricles. Two rubber diaphragms, designed to mimic the pumping action of the natural heart, were kept beating by an external compressor that was connected to the implant by hoses. This first recipient survived 112 days and died as a result of various physical complications caused by the implant. Subsequent patients fared little better or even worse, so that use of the Jarvik-7 was stopped. In 2001 a team of American surgeons implanted the first completely self-contained artificial heart, called the AbioCor artificial heart. The patient survived 151 days.

In 2008 a fully functional artificial heart was developed by Carmat, a French company founded by cardiologist Alain Carpentier. The device was covered with a specially designed biosynthetic material to prevent the development of blood clots and to reduce the likelihood of immune rejection—problems associated with the AbioCor and Jarvik-7 artificial hearts. The Carmat heart also utilized sensors to regulate blood flow and heartbeat. Plans to test the heart first in calves and sheep and later in humans with terminal heart failure were being developed.

Robert K. Jarvik developed the world's first artificial heart while working at the University of Utah in the 1970s. The Jarvik-7, which he is seen holding here, used two air-powered pumps.

PACEMAKERS

The pacemaker is an electronic cardiac-support device that produces rhythmic electrical impulses that take over the regulation of the heartbeat in patients with certain types of heart disease.

A healthy human heart contains its own electrical conducting system capable of controlling both the rate and the order of cardiac contractions. Electrical impulses are generated at the sinoatrial node in the right atrium, one of the two upper chambers of the heart. They then pass through the muscles of both atria to trigger the contraction of those two chambers, which forces blood into the ventricles. The wave of atrial electrical activity activates a second patch of conductive tissue, the atrioventricular node, initiating a second discharge along an assembly of conductive fibres called the bundle of His, which induces the contraction of the ventricles. When electrical conduction through the atrioventricular node or bundle of His is interrupted, the condition is called heart block. An artificial pacemaker may be employed temporarily until normal conduction returns or permanently to overcome the block.

In temporary pacing, a miniature electrode attached to fine wires is introduced into the heart through a vein, usually in the arm. The pacing device, an electric generator, remains outside the body and produces regular pulses of electric charge to maintain the heartbeat. In permanent pacing, the electrode

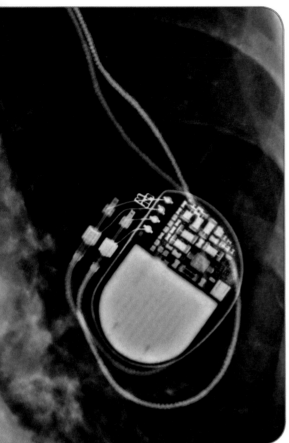

Implantable cardioverter defibrillators (ICDs) are imbedded into the chest to track a person's heart rate and deliver a jolt to correct it if necessary. Some ICDs also work as pacemakers.

may again be passed into the heart through a vein or it may be surgically implanted on the surface of the heart; in either case the electrode is generally located in the right ventricle. The electric generator is placed just beneath the skin, usually in a surgically created pocket below the collarbone.

The first pacemakers were of a type called asynchronous, or fixed, and they generated regular discharges that overrode the natural pacemaker. The rate of an asynchronous pacemaker may be altered by the physician, but once set it will continue to generate an electric pulse at regular intervals. Most are set at 70 to 75 beats per minute. More-recent devices are synchronous, or demand, pacemakers that trigger heart contractions only when the normal beat is interrupted. Most pacemakers of this type are designed to generate a pulse when the natural heart rate falls below 68 to 72 beats per minute.

Once in place, the electrode and wires of the pacemaker usually require almost no further attention. The power source of the implanted pulse generator, however, requires replacement at regular intervals, generally every four to five years. Most pacemakers use batteries as a power source.

Pacemakers designed to communicate wirelessly, using radio-frequency telemetry-based technology, have enabled physicians to gather information about a patient remotely. The implanted pacemakers transmit information to home monitoring systems and to programming devices used by doctors. As a result, a doctor working in a clinic can collect important information about a patient's heart function while the patient is at home. This type of wireless device also sends out alert signals to the physician when the patient's heart rate becomes abnormal.

DIALYSIS

Also called hemodialysis, renal dialysis, or kidney dialysis, dialysis is the process of removing blood from a patient whose kidney functioning is faulty, purifying that blood by dialysis, and returning it to the patient's bloodstream. The artificial kidney, or hemodialyzer, is a machine that provides a means for removing certain undesirable substances from the blood or of adding needed components to it. By these processes the apparatus can control the acid–base balance of the blood and its content of water and dissolved materials. Another known function of the natural kidney—secretion of hormones that influence the blood pressure—cannot be duplicated. Modern dialyzers rely on two physicochemical principles, dialysis and ultrafiltration.

In dialysis two liquids separated by a porous membrane exchange those components that exist as particles small enough to diffuse through the pores. When the blood is brought into contact with one side of such a membrane, dissolved substances (including urea and inorganic salts) pass through into a sterile solution placed on the other side of the membrane. The red and white cells, platelets, and proteins cannot penetrate the membrane because the particles are too large. To prevent or limit the loss of diffusible substances required by the body, such as sugars, amino acids, and necessary amounts of salts, those compounds are added to the sterile solution; thus their diffusion from the blood is offset by equal movement in the opposite direction. The lack of diffusible materials in the blood can be corrected by incorporating them in the solution, from which they enter the circulation.

Although water passes easily through the membrane, it is not removed by dialysis because its concentration in the blood is lower than in the solution; indeed, water tends to pass from the solution into the blood. The dilution of the blood that would result from this process is prevented by ultrafiltration, by which some of the water, along with some dissolved materials, is forced through the membrane by maintaining the blood at a higher pressure than the solution.

The membranes first used in dialysis were obtained from animals or prepared from collodion; cellophane has been found to be more suitable, and tubes or sheets of it are used in many dialyzers. In the late 1960s hollow filaments of cellulosic or synthetic materials were introduced for dialysis; bundles of such filaments provide a large membrane surface in a small volume, a combination advantageous in devising compact dialyzers.

Dialysis—which was first used to treat human patients in 1945—replaces or supplements the action of the kidneys in a person suffering from acute or chronic renal failure or from poisoning by diffusible substances, such as aspirin, bromides, or barbiturates. Blood is diverted from an artery, usually one in the wrist, into the dialyzer, where it flows—either by its own impetus or with the aid of a mechanical pump— along one surface of the membrane. Finally the blood passes through a trap that removes clots and bubbles and returns to a vein in the patient's forearm. In persons with chronic kidney failure, who require frequent dialysis, repeated surgical access to the blood

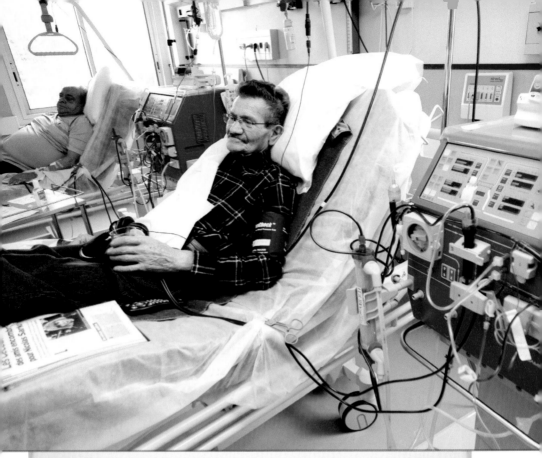

Patients who go to dialysis centres generally have three- to four-hour sessions three times a week. Those who receive dialysis at home tend to have shorter, more frequent sessions.

vessels used in the treatments is obviated by provision of an external plastic shunt between them.

BLADDER PACEMAKERS

Persons with a neurogenic bladder are able neither to urinate when their bladder is full nor, in some cases, to sense when it is full. They can be helped by an implant-able bladder pacemaker that senses when the bladder is full. The patient must use a hand-held control to activate an implanted pump that then immediately empties the bladder. The pacemaker has the added benefit of minimizing the likelihood of infection in the bladder, kidney, and urinary tract by eliminating the use of inserted catheters, or tubes, to empty the bladder.

THE EARS

Hearing aids are probably the most widely used sensory aids produced by biomedical engineering. These may contain either transistor amplifiers or tiny integrated circuits that amplify sound waves over much of the audible frequency range in humans (20 to 32,000 hertz). The amplified sound waves are conducted either through the skull or to the sound structures in the ear. Speech detection can also be done more efficiently by means of a computer chip. A program contained in a single computer chip can extract and amplify certain phonemes, or sound groups, from the nasal and vocal sounds of a person speaking to a hearing-impaired person who has such a chip implanted in his ear.

A cochlear implant is an electrical device inserted surgically into the human ear that enables the detection of sound in persons with severe hearing impairment. The cochlea is a coiled sensory structure in the inner ear that plays a fundamental role in hearing. It is innervated by the cochlear nerve, which branches from the larger vestibulocochlear nerve and serves as the primary fibre for the relay of electrical impulses carrying information about sound from the external environment to the auditory nucleus, or sound-processing centre, of the brain. Cochlear implants are most often used in adults affected by profound sensorineural deafness (hearing loss caused by damage to or congenital deformity of the inner ear), although children with this form of deafness who do not benefit from external hearing aids may also be candidates for cochlear implantation.

Modern cochlear implants have both external and internal components. External parts include a microphone, the tip of which rests just above the external auditory canal; a sound processor, which organizes sound detected by the microphone; and a transmitter, which consists of an electrical coil held in place by a magnet and conducts information via electromagnetic induction or radio frequency from the processor to a receiver/stimulator that lies beneath the skin. The receiver/stimulator is anchored in the temporal bone and is one of the two primary internal components of the cochlear device, the second being an electrode array that is implanted along the cochlear nerve fibre. The receiver/stimulator converts transmitter signals into electrical impulses, which are relayed along a cable to the electrode array. This mechanism of impulse conduction mimics the normal function of the cochlear nerve by stimulating nerve fibres that lead to the auditory nucleus.

Many patients with cochlear implants experience immediate improvements in hearing, and those who benefit most rapidly tend to be adults who lost their hearing after having already developed extensive language and speech skills. Young children who undergo intense therapy following implantation often make substantial gains in speech recognition and in their ability to discern different types of sound, including loud and soft sounds. Some individuals with cochlear implants eventually can even understand speech without lip reading. However, not all patients benefit to this extent, and a few actually may experience a complete loss of hearing in the affected ear as a result of the implantation procedure or the presence of the implant itself. Other side effects associated with the procedure or the device include infection, numbness around the ear, tinnitus (a constant ringing or buzzing noise in the ears), implant failure, and injury to the facial nerve, which runs through the temporal bone and passes close to the vestibulocochlear nerve. Surgical implantation of a cochlear device requires general anesthesia.

The first successful implantation of electrodes capable of stimulating the auditory nucleus was reported in 1957 by French otolaryngologists André Djourno and Charles Eyriès, who embedded electrodes near the cochlear nerve of a patient who was suffering from a condition known as cholesteatoma (the growth of a cyst in the middle ear that results in hearing loss). Later refinements in cochlear implant technologies led to the development of multichannel electrode arrays, which enable patients to sense different frequencies of complex sounds and to recognize speech patterns. Of particular significance was the multichannel implant technology invented by Australian physician Graeme Clark.

Advances in electrode technologies and device materials have reduced the risk of infection associated with cochlear implants. In addition, reductions in the sizes of external parts have given newer devices a relatively discreet appearance, although in young

In the late 20th century, cochlear implants were introduced as an aid for people with severe to complete hearing loss. This drawing shows one type of cochlear implant.

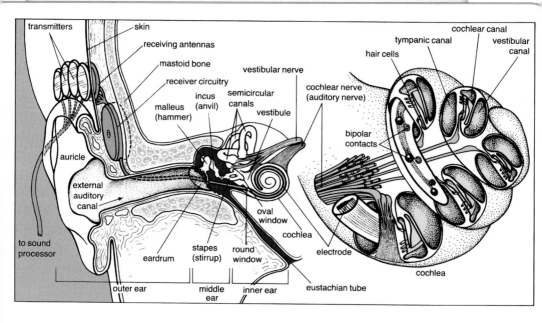

children the microphone and transmitter are often conspicuous. Despite these vast improvements in cochlear implant technology, however, the long-term effects of the electrodes on the nerves and function of the auditory nucleus remain unknown.

THE EYES

Artificial eyes have a long history. Until recently they were merely cosmetic, taking the place of badly damaged eyes but unable to help their wearers see in any way. However this is changing. Bioengineers have developed prosthetic eyes that can stimulate the ganglion cells in the eye's retina, improving the wearer's vision to some degree. Bioengineers hope to someday develop an artificial eye that will make it possible for the visually impaired to see clearly.

The process of implanting an artificial lens into a patient's eye is known as an intraocular lens (IOL) implant. Systomatic cataracts are generally treated by a surgery that involves the removal of the offending lens and placement of an artificial lens within the eye. A cataract is an opacity of the crystalline lens of the eye. Cataracts occur in 50 percent of people between the ages of 65 and 74 and in 70 percent of people over the age of 75. Typical age-related cataracts can cause cloudy vision, glare, colour vision problems, changes in eyeglass prescription, and, rarely, double vision (only in the affected eye). Usually, these types of cataracts are bilateral, although one eye may be more affected than the other.

The intraocular lenses used to treat patients with cataracts have evolved with time. The original IOLs were monofocal, or capable of correcting just long-distance vision, which meant people who got the implants generally needed glasses for reading and other up-close activities. However, today's bioengineers are developing multifocal IOLs, which can provide clear vision at different distances.

While intraocular lens implants are primarily used to correct cataracts, the same method can also be used to correct the focusing ability of the eye that causes myopia. These lenses are known as phakic intraocular lens implants.

CHAPTER 4

BIOMATERIALS

The treatment of many human disease conditions requires surgical intervention in order to assist, augment, sustain, or replace a diseased organ, and such procedures involve the use of materials foreign to the body. These materials, known as biomaterials, include synthetic polymers and, to a lesser extent, biological polymers, metals, and ceramics. Specific applications of biomaterials range from high-volume products such as blood bags, syringes, and needles to more challenging implantable devices designed to augment or replace a diseased human organ. The latter devices are used in cardiovascular, orthopedic, and dental applications as well as in a wide range of invasive treatment and diagnostic systems. Many of these devices have made possible notable clinical successes. For example, in cardiovascular applications,

Doctors can replace a damaged hip joint with an artificial joint. Artificial joints are generally made out of metal, ceramic, plastic, or a mix of these materials.

thousands of lives have been saved by heart valves, heart pacemakers, and large-diameter vascular grafts, and orthopedic hip-joint replacements have shown great long-term success in the treatment of patients suffering from debilitating joint diseases. With such a tremendous increase in medical applications, demand for a wide range of biomaterials grows by 5 to 15 percent each year. In the United States the annual market for surgical implants exceeds $10 billion, approximately 10 percent of world demand.

Nevertheless, applications of biomaterials are limited by biocompatibility, the problem of adverse interactions arising at the junction between the biomaterial and the host tissue. Optimizing the interactions that occur at the surface of implanted biomaterials represents the most significant key to further advances, and an excellent basis for these advances can be found in the growing understanding of complex biological materials and in the development of novel biomaterials custom-designed at the molecular level for specific medical applications.

GENERAL REQUIREMENTS OF BIOMATERIALS

Research on developing new biomaterials is an interdisciplinary effort, often involving collaboration among materials scientists and engineers, biomedical engineers, pathologists, and clinicians to solve clinical problems. The design or selection of a specific biomaterial depends on the relative importance of the various properties that are required for the intended medical application. Physical properties that are generally considered include hardness, tensile strength, modulus, and elongation; fatigue strength, which is determined by a material's response to cyclic loads or strains; impact properties; resistance to abrasion and wear; long-term dimensional stability, which is described by a material's viscoelastic properties; swelling in aqueous media; and permeability to gases, water, and small biomolecules. In addition, biomaterials are exposed to human tissues and fluids, so that predicting the results of possible interactions between host and material is an important and unique consideration in using synthetic materials in medicine. Two particularly important issues in biocompatibility are thrombosis, which involves blood coagulation and the adhesion of blood platelets to bio-material surfaces, and the fibrous-tissue encapsulation of biomaterials that are implanted in soft tissues.

Poor selection of materials can lead to clinical problems. One example of this situation was the choice of silicone rubber as a poppet in an early heart valve design. The silicone absorbed lipid from plasma and swelled sufficiently to become trapped between the metal struts of the valve. Another unfortunate choice as a biomaterial was Teflon (trademark), which is noted for its low coefficient of friction and its chemical inertness but which has relatively poor abrasion resistance. Thus, as an occluder in a heart valve or as an acetabular cup in a hip-joint prosthesis, Teflon may eventually wear to such an extent that the device would fail. In addition, degradable polyester-urethane foam was abandoned as a fixation patch for breast prostheses, because it offered a distinct possibility for the release of carcinogenic by-products as it degraded.

Besides their constituent polymer molecules, synthetic biomaterials may contain several additives, such as unreacted monomers and catalysts, inorganic fillers or organic plasticizers, antioxidants and stabilizers, and processing lubricants or mold-release agents on the material's surface. In addition, several degradation products may result from the processing, sterilization, storage, and ultimately implantation of a device. Many additives are beneficial—for example, the silica filler that is indispensable in silicone rubber for good mechanical performance or the antioxidants and stabilizers that prevent premature oxidative degradation of polyetherurethanes. Other additives, such as pigments, can be eliminated from biomedical products. Indeed, a "medical-grade" biomaterial is one that has had nonessential additives and potential contaminants excluded or eliminated from the polymer. In order to achieve this grade, the polymer may need to be solvent-extracted before use, thereby eliminating low-molecular-weight materials. Generally, additives in polymers are regarded with extreme suspicion, because it is often the additives rather than the constituent polymer molecules that are the source of adverse biocompatibility.

POLYMER BIOMATERIALS

The majority of biomaterials used in humans are synthetic polymers such as the polyurethanes or Dacron (trademark; chemical name polyethylene terephthalate), rather than polymers of biological origin such as proteins or polysaccharides. The properties of common synthetic biomaterials vary widely, from the soft and delicate water-absorbing

POLYMERS

A polymer is any of a class of natural or synthetic substances composed of very large molecules, called macromolecules, that are multiples of simpler chemical units called monomers. Polymers make up many of the materials in living organisms, including, for example, proteins, cellulose, and nucleic acids. Moreover, they constitute the basis of such minerals as diamond, quartz, and feldspar and such man-made materials as concrete, glass, paper, plastics, and rubbers.

The word "polymer" designates an unspecified number of monomer units. When the number of monomers is very large, the compound is sometimes called a high polymer. Polymers are not restricted to monomers of the same chemical composition or molecular weight and structure. Some natural polymers are composed of one kind of monomer. Most natural and synthetic polymers, however, are made up of two or more different types of monomers. Such polymers are known as copolymers.

Organic polymers play a crucial role in living things, providing basic structural materials and participating in vital life processes. For example, the solid parts of all plants are made up of polymers. These include cellulose, lignin, and various resins. Cellulose is a polysaccharide, a polymer that is composed of sugar molecules. Lignin consists of a complicated three-dimensional network of polymers. Wood resins are polymers of a simple hydrocarbon, isoprene. Another familiar isoprene polymer is rubber.

Other important natural polymers include the proteins, which are polymers of amino acids, and the nucleic acids, which are polymers of nucleotides—complex molecules composed of nitrogen-containing bases, sugars, and phosphoric acid. The nucleic acids carry genetic information in the cell. Starches, important sources of food energy derived from plants, are natural polymers composed of glucose.

hydrogels made into contact lenses to the resilient elastomers found in short- and long-term cardiovascular devices or the high-strength acrylics used in orthopedics and dentistry. The properties of any material are governed by its chemical composition and by the intra- and intermolecular forces that dictate its molecular organization. Macromolecular structure in turn affects macroscopic properties and, ultimately, the interfacial behaviour of the material in contact with blood or host tissues.

Since the properties of each material are dependent on the chemical structure and macromolecular organization of its polymer chains, an understanding of some common structural features of various polymers provides considerable insight into their properties. Compared with complex biological molecules, synthetic polymers are relatively simple; often they comprise only one type of repeating subunit, analogous to a polypeptide consisting of just one repeating amino acid. On the basis of common structures and properties, synthetic polymers are classified into one of three categories: elastomers, which include natural and synthetic rubbers;

thermoplastics; and thermosets. The properties that provide the basis for this classification include molecular weight, cross-link density, percent crystallinity, thermal transition temperature, and bulk mechanical properties.

ELASTOMERS

Elastomers, which include rubber materials, have found wide use as biomaterials in cardiovascular and soft-tissue applications owing to their high elasticity, impact resistance, and gas permeability. Applications of elastomers include flexible tubing for pacemaker leads, vascular grafts, and catheters; biocompatible coatings and pumping diaphragms for artificial hearts and left-ventricular assist devices; grafts for reconstructive surgery and maxillofacial operations; wound dressings; breast prostheses; and membranes for implantable biosensors.

Elastomers are typically amorphous with low cross-link density (although linear polyurethane block copolymers are an important exception). This gives them low to moderate modulus and tensile properties as well as high elasticity. For example, elastomeric devices can be extended by 100 to 1,000 percent of their initial dimensions without causing any permanent deformation to the material. Silicone rubbers such as Silastic (trademark), produced by the American manufacturer Dow Corning, Inc., are cross-linked, so that they cannot be melted or dissolved—although swelling may occur in the presence of a good solvent. Such properties contrast

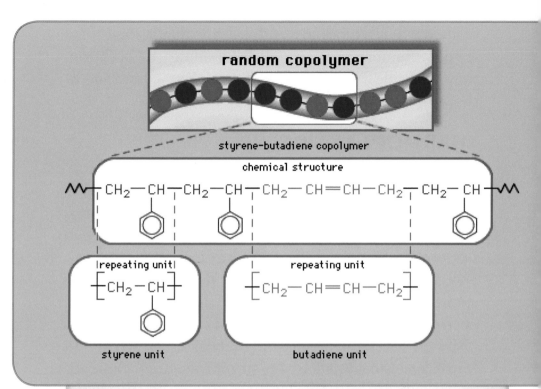

This diagram shows the random arrangement of styrene and butadiene units in a styrene-butadiene copolymer (SBR). This elastomer is a general-purpose synthetic rubber.

with those of the linear polyurethane elastomers, which consist of soft polyether amorphous segments and hard urethane-containing glassy or crystalline segments. The two segments are incompatible at room temperature and undergo microphase separation, forming hard domains dispersed in an amorphous matrix. A key feature of this macromolecular organization is that the hard domains serve as physical cross-links and reinforcing filler. This results in elastomeric materials that possess relatively high modulus and extraordinary long-term stability under sustained cyclic loading. In addition, they can be processed by methods common to thermoplastics.

THERMOPLASTICS

Many common thermoplastics, such as polyethylene and polyester, are used as biomaterials. Thermoplastics usually exhibit moderate to high tensile strength (5 to 1,000 megapascals) with moderate elongation (2 to 100 percent), and they undergo plastic deformation at high strains. Thermoplastics consist of linear or branched polymer chains; consequently, most can undergo reversible melt-solid transformation on heating, which allows for relatively easy processing or reprocessing. Depending on the structure and molecular organization of the polymer chains, thermoplastics may be amorphous (e.g., polystyrene), semicrystalline (e.g., low-density polyethylene), or highly crystalline (e.g., high-density polyethylene), or they may be processed into highly crystalline textile fibres (e.g., polyester Dacron).

Some thermoplastic biomaterials, such as polylactic acid and polyglycolic acid, are polymers based on a repeating amino acid subunit. These polypeptides are biodegradable, and, along with biodegradable polyesters and polyorthoesters, they have applications in absorbable sutures and drug-release systems. The rate of biodegradation in the body can be adjusted by using copolymers. These are polymers that link two different monomer subunits into a single polymer chain. The resultant biomaterial exhibits properties, including biodegradation, that are intermediate between the two homopolymers.

THERMOSETS

Thermosetting polymers find only limited application in medicine, but their characteristic properties, which combine high strength and chemical resistance, are useful for some orthopedic and dental devices. Thermosetting polymers such as epoxies and acrylics are chemically inert, and they also have high modulus and tensile properties with negligible elongation (1 to 2 percent). The polymer chains in these materials are highly cross-linked and therefore have severely restricted macromolecular mobility; this limits extension of the polymer chains under an applied load. As a result, thermosets are strong but brittle materials.

Cross-linking inhibits close packing of polymer chains, preventing formation of crystalline regions. Another consequence of extensive cross-linking is that thermosets do not undergo solid-melt transformation on heating, so that they cannot be melted or reprocessed.

APPLICATIONS OF BIOMATERIALS

Two of the most common uses of biomaterials are in orthopedic devices and cardiovascular devices. Biomaterials are used in many blood-contacting devices. These include artificial heart valves, synthetic vascular grafts, ventricular assist devices, drug-release systems, extracorporeal systems, and a wide range of invasive treatment and diagnostic systems.

Joint replacements, particularly at the hip, and bone fixation devices have become very successful applications of materials in medicine. The use of pins, plates, and screws for bone fixation to aid recovery of bone fractures has become routine, with the number of annual procedures approaching five million in the United States alone. In joint replacement, typical patients are age 55 or older and suffer from debilitating rheumatoid arthritis, osteoarthritis, or osteoporosis. Orthopedic surgeries for artificial joints exceed 1.5 million each year, with actual joint replacement accounting for about half of the procedures. A major focus of research is the development of new biomaterials for artificial joints intended for younger, more active patients.

CARDIOVASCULAR DEVICES

An important issue in the design and selection of materials for cardiovascular devices is the hemodynamic conditions in the vicinity of the device. For example, mechanical heart valve implants are intended for long-term use. Consequently, the hinge points of each valve leaflet and the materials must have excellent wear and fatigue resistance in order to open and close 80 times per minute for many years after implantation. In addition, the open valve must minimize disturbances to blood flow as blood passes from the left ventricle of the heart, through the heart valve, and into the ascending aorta of the arterial vascular system. To this end, the bileaflet valve disks of one type of implant are coated with pyrolytic carbon, which provides a relatively smooth, chemically inert surface. This is an important property, because surface roughness will cause turbulence in the blood flow, which in turn may lead to hemolysis of red cells, provide sites for adventitious bacterial adhesion and subsequent colonization, and, in areas of blood stasis, promote thrombosis and blood coagulation. The carbon-coated holding ring of this implant is covered with Dacron mesh fabric so that the surgeon can sew and fix the device to adjacent cardiac tissues. Furthermore, the porous structure of the Dacron mesh promotes tissue integration, which occurs over a period of weeks after implantation.

While the possibility of thrombosis can be minimized in blood-contacting biomaterials, it cannot be eliminated entirely. For this reason, patients who receive artificial heart valves or other blood-contacting devices also receive anticoagulation therapy. This is needed

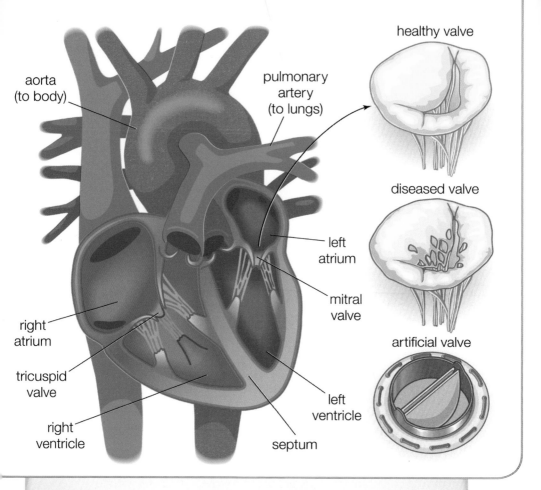

aorta
(to body)

pulmonary
artery
(to lungs)

healthy valve

diseased valve

left
atrium

mitral
valve

right
atrium

tricuspid
valve

right
ventricle

septum

left
ventricle

artificial valve

One, two, or even three diseased heart valves can be replaced with artificial valves made of stainless steel, Dacron, or other special materials.

because all foreign surfaces initiate blood coagulation and platelet adhesion to some extent. Platelets are circulating cellular components of blood, two to four micrometres in size, that attach to foreign surfaces and actively participate in blood coagulation and thrombus formation. Research on new biomaterials for cardiovascular applications is largely devoted to understanding thrombus formation and to developing novel surfaces for biomaterials that will provide improved blood compatibility.

Synthetic vascular graft materials are used to patch injured or diseased areas of arteries, for replacement of whole segments of larger arteries such as the aorta, and for use as sewing cuffs (as with the heart valve mentioned above). Such materials need to be flexible to allow for the difficulties of implantation and to avoid irritating adjacent tissues; also, the internal diameter of the graft should remain constant under a wide range of flexing and bending conditions, and the modulus or compliance of the vessel should be similar to that of the natural vessel. These aims are largely achieved by crimped woven Dacron and expanded polytetrafluoro-ethylene (ePTFE). Crimping of Dacron in processing results in a porous vascular graft that may be bent $180°$ or twisted without collapsing the internal diameter.

A biomaterial used for blood vessel replacement will be in contact not only with blood but also with adjacent soft tissues. Experience with different materials has shown that tissue growth into the interstices of the biomaterials aids healing and integration of the material with host tissue after implantation. In order for the tissue, which consists mostly of collagen, to grow in the graft, the vascular graft must have an open structure with pores at least 10 micrometres in diameter. These pores allow new blood capillaries that develop during healing to grow into the graft, and the blood then provides oxygen and other nutrients for fibroblasts and other cells to survive in the biomaterial matrix. Fibroblasts synthesize the structural protein tropocollagen, which is needed in the development of new fibrous tissue as part of the healing response to a surgical wound.

Occasionally, excessive tissue growth may be observed at the anastomosis, which is where the graft is sewn to the native artery. This is referred to as internal hyperplasia and is thought to result from differences in compliance between the graft and the host vessels. In addition, in order to optimize compatibility of the biomaterial with the blood, the synthetic graft eventually should be coated with a confluent layer of host endothelial cells, but this does not occur with current materials. Therefore, most proposed modifications to existing graft materials involve potential improvements in blood compatibility.

Artificial heart valves and vascular grafts, while not ideal, have been used successfully and have saved many thousands of lives. However, the risk of thrombosis has limited the success of existing cardiovascular devices and has restricted potential application of the biomaterials to other devices. For example, there is an urgent clinical need for blood-compatible, synthetic vascular grafts of small diameter in peripheral vascular surgery—e.g., in the legs—but this is currently impracticable with existing biomaterials because of the high risk of thrombotic occlusion. Similarly, progress with implantable miniature sensors, designed to measure a wide range of blood conditions continuously, has been impeded because of problems directly attributable to the failure of existing biomaterials. With such biocompatibility problems resolved, biomedical sensors would provide a very important contribution to medical diagnosis and monitoring. Considerable advances have been made in the ability to manipulate molecular architecture at the surfaces of materials by using chemisorbed or physisorbed monolayer films. Such progress in surface modification, combined with the development of nanoscale probes that permit examination at the molecular and submolecular level, provide a strong basis for optimism in the development of specialty biomaterials with improved blood compatibility.

ORTHOPEDIC DEVICES

Hip-joint replacements are principally used for structural support. Consequently, they are dominated by materials that possess high strength, such as metals, tough plastics, and reinforced polymer-matrix composites. In addition, biomaterials used for orthopedic applications must have high modulus, long-term dimensional stability, high fatigue resistance, long-term biostability, excellent abrasion resistance, and biocompatibility (i.e., there should be no adverse tissue response to the implanted device). Early developments in this field used readily available materials such as stainless steels, but evidence of corrosion after implantation led to their replacement by more stable materials, particularly titanium alloys, cobalt-chromium-molybdenum alloys, and carbon fibre-reinforced polymer composites. A typical modern artificial hip consists of a nitrided and highly polished cobalt-chromium ball connected to a titanium alloy stem that is inserted into the femur and cemented into place by in situ polymerization of polymethylmethacrylate. The articulating component of the joint consists of an acetabular cup made of tough, creep-resistant, ultrahigh-molecular-weight polyethylene. Abrasion at the ball-and-cup interface can lead to the production of wear particles, which in turn can lead to significant inflammatory reaction by the host. Consequently, much research on the development of hip-joint materials has been devoted to optimizing the properties of the articulating components in order to eliminate surface wear. Other modifications include porous coatings made by sintering the metal surface or coatings of wire mesh or hydroxyapatite; these promote bone growth and integration between the implant and the host, eliminating the need for an acrylic bone cement.

While the strength of the biomaterials is important, another goal is to match the mechanical properties of the implant materials with those of the bone in order to provide a uniform distribution of stresses (load sharing). If a bone is loaded insufficiently, the stress distribution will be made asymmetric, and this will lead to adaptive remodeling with cortical thinning

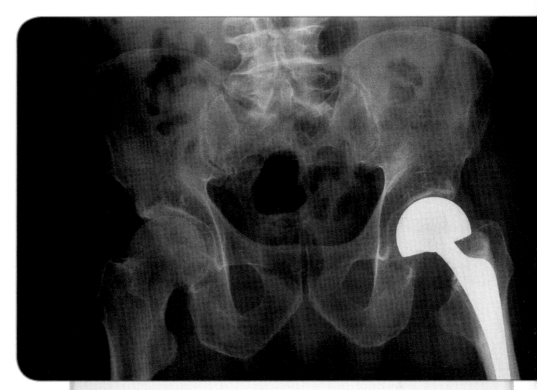

An X-ray showing an artificial hip. Since the hip is a ball-and-joint socket, it is important that the elements composing it can move easily and smoothly against each other.

and increased porosity of the bone. Such lessons in structure hierarchy and in the structure-property relationships of materials have been obtained from studies on biologic composite materials, and they are being translated into new classes of synthetic biomaterials. One development is carbon fibre-reinforced polymer-matrix composites. Typical matrix polymers include polysulfone and polyetheretherketones. The strength of these composites is lower than that of metals, but it more closely approximates that of bone.

NANOTECHNOLOGY

Some of today's biggest advances in biomaterials and biotechnology are happening on a very small scale. Nanotechnology is the manipulation and manufacture of materials and devices on the scale of atoms or small groups of atoms. It promises to impact medical treatment in multiple ways.

The "nanoscale" is typically measured in nanometres, or billionths of a metre (*nanos*, the Greek word for "dwarf," being the source of the prefix), and materials built at this scale often exhibit distinctive physical and chemical properties due to quantum mechanical effects. Although usable devices this small may be decades away, techniques for working at the nanoscale have become essential to electronic engineering, and nanoengineered materials have begun to appear in consumer products. For example, billions of microscopic "nanowhiskers," each about 10 nanometres in length, have been molecularly hooked onto natural and synthetic fibres to impart stain resistance to clothing and other fabrics; zinc oxide nanocrystals have been used to create invisible sunscreens that block ultraviolet light; and silver nanocrystals have been embedded in bandages to kill bacteria and prevent infection.

Possibilities for the future are numerous. Nanotechnology may make it possible to manufacture lighter, stronger, and programmable materials that require less energy to produce than conventional materials and that produce less waste than with conventional manufacturing. Nanocoatings for both opaque and translucent surfaces may render them resistant to corrosion, scratches, and radiation. Nanoscale electronic, magnetic, and mechanical devices and systems with unprecedented levels of information processing may be fabricated, as may chemical, photochemical, and biological sensors for protection, health care, manufacturing, and the environment. The potential for improvements in health, safety, quality of life, and conservation of the environment are vast.

DRUG DELIVERY

Advances in nanoscale particle design and fabrication provide new options for drug delivery and drug therapies. More than half of the new drugs developed each year are not water-soluble, which makes their delivery difficult. In the form of nanosized particles, however, these drugs are more readily transported to their destination, and they can be delivered in the conventional form of pills.

More important, nanotechnology may enable drugs to be delivered to precisely the right location in the body and to release drug doses on a predetermined schedule for optimal treatment. The general approach is to attach the drug to a nanosized carrier that will release the medicine in the body over an extended period of time or when specifically triggered to do so. In addition, the surfaces of these nanoscale carriers may be treated to seek out and become localized at a disease site—for example, attaching to cancerous tumours. One type of molecule of special interest for these applications is an organic dendrimer. A dendrimer is a special class of polymeric molecule that weaves in and out from a hollow central region. These spherical "fuzz balls" are about the size of a typical protein but cannot unfold like proteins. Interest in dendrimers derives from the ability to tailor their cavity sizes and chemical properties to hold different therapeutic agents. Researchers hope to design different dendrimers that can swell and release their drug on exposure to specifically recognized molecules that indicate a disease target. This same general approach to nanoparticle-directed drug delivery is being explored for other types of nanoparticles as well.

Another approach involves gold-coated nano-shells whose size can be adjusted to absorb light energy at different wavelengths. In particular, infrared light will pass through several centimetres of body tissue, allowing a delicate and precise heating of such capsules in order to release the therapeutic substance within. Furthermore, antibodies may be attached to the outer gold surface of the shells to cause them to bind specifically to certain tumour cells, thereby reducing the damage to surrounding healthy cells.

BIOASSAYS

A second area of intense study in nanomedicine is that of developing new diagnostic tools. Motivation for this work ranges from fundamental biomedical research at the level of single genes or cells to point-of-care applications for health delivery services. With advances in molecular biology, much diagnostic work now focuses on detecting specific biological "signatures." These analyses are referred to as bioassays. Examples include studies to determine which genes are active in response to a particular disease or drug therapy. A general approach involves attaching fluorescing dye molecules to the target biomolecules in order to reveal their concentration.

Another approach to bioassays uses semiconductor nanoparticles, such as cadmium selenide, which emit light of a specific wavelength depending on their size. Different-size particles can be tagged to different receptors so that a wider variety of distinct colour tags are available than can be distinguished for dye molecules. The degradation in fluorescence with repeated excitation for dyes is avoided. Furthermore, various-size particles can be encapsulated in latex beads and their resulting wavelengths read like a bar code. This approach, while still in the exploratory stage, would allow for an enormous number of distinct labels for bioassays.

Another nanotechnology variation on bioassays is to attach one half of the single-stranded complementary DNA segment for the genetic sequence to be detected to one set of gold particles and the other half to a second set of gold particles. When the material of interest is present in a solution, the two attachments cause the gold balls to agglomerate, providing a large change in

This scientist is using a bioassay to determine which species of Salmonella bacteria is present in a sample. Salmonella is transmitted mainly through contaminated food products, such as eggs and raw poultry.

optical properties that can be seen in the colour of the solution. If both halves of the sequence do not match, no agglomeration will occur and no change will be observed.

Approaches that do not involve optical detection techniques are also being explored with nanoparticles. For example, magnetic nanoparticles can be attached to antibodies that in turn recognize and attach to specific biomolecules. The magnetic particles then act as tags and "handlebars" through which magnetic fields can be used for mixing, extracting, or identifying the attached biomolecules within microlitre- or nanolitre-

sized samples. For example, magnetic nanoparticles stay magnetized as a single domain for a significant period, which enables them to be aligned and detected in a magnetic field. In particular, attached antibody–magnetic-nanoparticle combinations rotate slowly and give a distinctive magnetic signal. In contrast, magnetically tagged antibodies that are not attached to the biological material being detected rotate more rapidly and so do not give the same distinctive signal.

Microfluidic systems, or "labs-on-chips," have been developed for biochemical assays of minuscule samples. Typically cramming numerous electronic

95

and mechanical components into a portable unit no larger than a credit card, they are especially useful for conducting rapid analysis in the field. While these microfluidic systems primarily operate at the microscale (that is, millionths of a metre), nanotechnology has contributed new concepts and will likely play an increasing role in the future. For example, separation of DNA is sensitive to entropic effects, such as the entropy required to unfold DNA of a given length. A new approach to separating DNA could take advantage of its passage through a nanoscale array of posts or channels such that DNA molecules of different lengths would uncoil at different rates.

Other researchers have focused on detecting signal changes as nanometre-wide DNA strands are threaded through a nanoscale pore. Early studies used pores punched in membranes by viruses; artificially fabricated nanopores are also being tested. By applying an electric potential across the membrane in a liquid cell to pull the DNA through, changes in ion current can be measured as different repeating base units of the molecule pass through the pores. Nanotechnology-enabled advances in the entire area of bioassays will clearly impact health care in many ways, from early detection, rapid clinical analysis, and home monitoring to new understanding of molecular biology and genetic-based treatments for fighting disease.

ASSISTIVE DEVICES AND TISSUE ENGINEERING

Another biomedical application of nanotechnology involves assistive devices for people who have lost or lack certain natural capabilities. For example, researchers hope to design retinal implants for vision-impaired individuals. The concept is to implant chips with photodetector arrays to transmit signals from the retina to the brain via the optic nerve. Meaningful spatial information, even if only at a rudimentary level, would be of great assistance to the blind.

Closely related research involves implanting nanoscale neural probes in brain tissue to activate and control motor functions. This requires effective and stable "wiring" of many electrodes to neurons. It is exciting because of the possibility of recovery of control for motor-impaired individuals. Studies employing neural stimulation of damaged spinal cords by electrical signals have demonstrated the return of some locomotion. Researchers are also seeking ways to assist in the regeneration and healing of bone, skin, and cartilage—for example, developing synthetic biocompatible or biodegradable structures with nanosized voids that would serve as templates for regenerating specific tissue while delivering chemicals to assist in the repair process. At a more sophisticated level, researchers hope to someday build nanoscale or microscale machines that can repair, assist, or replace more-complex organs.

CHAPTER 5

SUBFIELDS OF BIOENGINEERING

S ince bioengineering is such a rapidly evolving field, it is not surprising that new subfields are constantly emerging. New related fields are likewise emerging. At the same time, existing fields are increasingly overlapping with bioengineering. The line separating subfields and related fields from bioengineering—or even from each other—can be vague. This chapter examines some subfields of bioengineering and explores genetic engineering, which is concerned with the artificial manipulation, modification, and recombination of deoxyribonucleic acid (DNA) or other nucleic acid molecules in order to modify an organism. The techniques employed in genetic engineering have led to the production of medically important products, including human insulin, human growth hormone, and hepatitis B vaccine.

The bioartificial tissue this scientist is holding was produced by "printing," or layering, a mix of living cells and a polymer onto a prepared surface called a tissue scaffold.

One field that is increasingly overlapping with bioengineering is biomechanics, the study of biological systems—particularly their structure and function—using methods derived from mechanics, which is concerned with the effects that forces have on the motion of bodies. Biochemical engineering is the application of engineering principles to microscopic biological systems that are used to create new products by synthesis, including the production of protein from suitable raw materials. The main objective of synthetic biology is to create fully operational biological systems from the smallest constituent parts possible, including DNA, proteins, and other organic molecules. Bionics is the study of living systems so that the knowledge gained can be applied to the design of physical systems. Biology meets information science in bioinformatics, the science of gathering and analyzing biological data on a large scale. Agricultural engineering includes the application of engineering principles to the problems of biological production and to the external operations and environment that influence this production. Environmental engineering, also called bioenvironmental engineering or environmental health engineering, concerns the application of engineering principles to the control of the environment for the health, comfort, and safety of humans.

SUBFIELDS OF BIOMEDICAL ENGINEERING

While biomedical engineering has many subfields, many of the most significant recent developments have been in the areas of tissue engineering—sometimes known as cell and tissue engineering—and neural engineering. Tissue engineering deals with the development of biological substitutes that can replace diseased or damaged human tissue. Also called neuroengineering, neural engineering is a discipline in which engineering technologies and mathematical and computational methods are combined with techniques in neuroscience and biology.

TISSUE ENGINEERING

Some of the most spectacular advances in recent years have been in the area of tissue engineering. These include artificial skin, bone marrow, and blood cells. Tissue engineering integrates engineering principles and synthetic materials with biological components, such as cells and growth factors. Scientists begin producing substitute tissues by seeding human cells onto scaffolds, which may be made from collagen or from a biodegradable polymer. The scaffolds are then incubated in mediums containing growth factors, which stimulate the cells to grow and divide. As cells spread across the scaffold, the substitute tissue is formed. This tissue can be implanted into the human body, with the implanted scaffold eventually being either absorbed or dissolved.

Skin, cartilage, heart, and bone are among the many tissues that are candidates for tissue engineering. The production of skin substitutes has played an important role in improving the success of skin graft surgeries, especially for complex wounds such as burns. Substitute tissues of the renal system, including urinary bladders and urethras, have also been engineered and transplanted successfully, thereby broadening therapeutic opportunities for complicated renal disorders.

NEURAL ENGINEERING

Objectives of neural engineering include the enhancement of understanding of the functions of the human nervous system and the improvement of human performance, especially after injury or disease. The field is multidisciplinary in that it draws from the neurological sciences (especially neurobiology and neurology) as well as from a diverse range of engineering disciplines, including computer sciences, robotics, material sciences, signal processing, and systems modeling and simulation. The field covers a variety of subjects and applications; examples include brain-computer interfaces, neuroimaging, neuroinformatics, neural tissue engineering, and neurorobotics.

While the potential applications of neural engineering are broad, the discipline offers particular opportunities for improving motor and sensory function after major injury to the human central nervous system, such as that caused by stroke, traumatic brain injury, or spinal cord injury. For those conditions, new technologies can be applied to help reroute neural signals around damaged areas of the brain or spinal cord or to substitute one type of neural signal for another type that is lost after the injury.

Animal models that were developed in the field have enabled researchers to study recordings from various cortical areas during normal voluntary behaviours, which has provided insight into human neural pathways.

Neural signals can be filtered and processed and then used to instruct computers, to control simple robotic devices, or to activate electrical stimulators to control limb muscles. Alternative approaches allow signals from skin or other sensory areas to be routed around damaged areas and to be delivered to the cerebral cortex by other means. For example, sensory signals from the eye or from skin can be detected by a range of electronic sensors and delivered to the cortex in the form of electrical stimulus trains.

Other developments in the field include advances in neural tissue engineering, which is aimed at the repair and regeneration of nerves; advances in neural recording systems that allow long-term recording from small groups of nerve fibres in peripheral muscle or skin nerves; and the development of implantable stimulators for use in promoting recovery of walking in individuals with spinal cord injury or for the restoration of motor function after cortical damage sustained as a result of stroke. For example, neural cuffs that are implanted around nerves innervating the foot sole can be used to sense foot contact during walking or to detect other phases of locomotion, allowing accurate programming of muscle nerve stimulation.

GENETIC ENGINEERING

Almost every living cell holds a vast storehouse of information encoded in genes, segments of deoxyribonucleic acid (DNA) that control how the cell replicates and functions and control the expression of inherited traits. The artificial manipulation of one or more genes in order to modify an organism is called genetic engineering.

The term "genetic engineering" initially encompassed all of the methods used for modifying organisms through heredity and reproduction. These included selective breeding, or artificial selection, as well as a wide range of biomedical techniques such as artificial insemination, in vitro fertilization, and gene manipulation. Today, however, the term is used to refer to the latter technique, specifically the field of recombinant DNA technology. In this process DNA molecules from two or more sources are combined and then inserted into a host organism, such as a bacterium. Inside the host cell the inserted, or foreign, DNA replicates and functions along with the host DNA.

Recombinant DNA technology has produced many new genetic combinations that have had great impact on science, medicine, agriculture, and industry. Despite the tremendous advances afforded to society through this technology, however, the practice is not without controversy. Special concern has been focused on the use of microorganisms in recombinant technology, with the worry that some genetic changes could introduce unfavorable and possibly dangerous traits, such as antibiotic resistance or toxin production, into microbes that were previously free of these.

HISTORY OF GENETIC ENGINEERING

Genetic engineering had its origins during the late 1960s in experiments with bacteria, viruses, and plasmids, small, free-floating rings of DNA found in bacteria. A key discovery was made by Swiss microbiologist Werner Arber, who in 1968 discovered restriction enzymes. These are naturally occurring enzymes that cut DNA into fragments during replication. A year later American biologist Hamilton O. Smith revealed that one type of restriction enzyme cut DNA at very specific points in the molecule. This enzyme was named type II restriction enzyme to distinguish it from type I and type III enzymes, which cut DNA in a different manner. In the early 1970s American biologist Daniel Nathans demonstrated that type II enzymes could be used to manipulate genes for research. For their efforts Smith, Nathans, and Arber were awarded the 1978 Nobel Prize for Physiology or Medicine.

The true fathers of genetic engineering were American biochemists Stanley Cohen and Herbert Boyer, who were the first scientists to use restriction enzymes to produce a genetically modified organism. In 1973 they used type II enzymes to cut DNA into fragments, recombine the fragments in vitro, and then insert the foreign genes into a common laboratory strain of bacteria. The foreign genes replicated along with the bacteria's genome; furthermore, the modified bacteria produced the proteins specified by the foreign DNA. The new age of biotechnology had begun.

HOW GENETIC ENGINEERING WORKS

The action of restriction enzymes—also called restriction endonucleases—is the crux of genetic engineering. These enzymes are found only in bacteria, where they protect the host genome against invading foreign DNA, such as a virus. Each restriction enzyme recognizes a short, specific sequence of nucleotide bases in the DNA molecule. These regions, called recognition sequences, are randomly distributed throughout the DNA molecule. Different bacterial species make restriction enzymes that recognize different nucleotide sequences. By convention, restriction enzymes are named for the genus, species, and strain designations of the bacteria that produce them and for the order in which they were first identified. For example, the enzyme EcoRI was the first restriction enzyme isolated from the *Escherichia coli* (*E. coli*) strain RY13.

Of the three types of restriction enzymes, type II is the most useful in genetic engineering. Types I and III restriction enzymes cleave DNA randomly, often at some distance from the recognition sequence. By contrast, type II restriction enzymes cut DNA at specific sites within the recognition sequence. Each time a particular restriction enzyme is used, the DNA is cut at precisely the same places in the molecule. Today more than 3,600 type II restriction enzymes are known, forming a molecular tool kit that allows scientists to cut chromosomes into various desired lengths, depending on how many different restriction enzymes are mixed with the chromosome under investigation.

At the cleavage site, different restriction enzymes cut DNA in one of two ways. Some enzymes make incisions in each strand at points immediately opposite each other, producing "blunt end" DNA fragments. Most

"Sticky ends" are not actually sticky. The term denotes that the overhang allows these fragments to bind more readily with other strands. Blunt ends are more difficult to join.

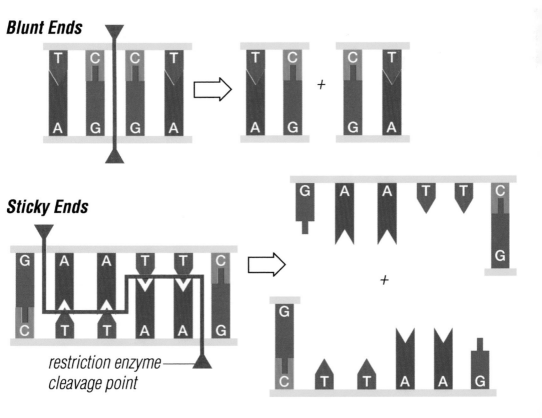

Blunt Ends

Sticky Ends

restriction enzyme cleavage point

enzymes cut the two strands at points not directly opposite each other, producing an overhang in each strand. These are called "sticky ends" because they readily pair with complementary bases on another fragment.

Genetic engineers use restriction enzymes to remove a gene from a donor organism's chromosome and insert it into a vector, a molecule of DNA that will function as a carrier. Plasmids are the most common vectors used in genetic engineering. These are circular DNA molecules found in some bacteria; they are extrachromosomal molecules, meaning that they replicate independently of the bacterial chromosome. The first step in the process involves mixing the donor organism's DNA with a set of restriction enzymes that will isolate the gene of interest by cutting it from its chromosome. In a separate step, a plasmid is cut with the same restriction enzymes. The donor gene DNA is then spliced into the plasmid, producing a recombinant DNA (rDNA) molecule that will function as a vector, which is introduced into bacterial cells. Inside the host cells, the plasmids replicate when the bacteria replicate. Because this produces many copies of the recombinant DNA molecule, recombinant DNA technology is often called gene cloning. In addition, when the bacteria's DNA initiates protein synthesis, the protein coded for by the inserted gene is produced.

GENETIC ENGINEERING IN MEDICINE

Medicine was the first area to benefit from genetic engineering. Using recombinant DNA technology, scientists can produce large quantities of many medically useful substances, including hormones, immune-system proteins, and proteins involved in blood clotting and blood-cell production. Before the advent of genetic engineering, many therapeutic peptides such as insulin were harvested from human cadavers and the pancreases of donor animals such as pigs or horses. Using foreign (nonhuman) proteins posed serious risks: in some patients the introduction of foreign proteins elicited serious allergic or immune reactions. Furthermore, there was a great risk of inadvertently transmitting viruses from the donor tissue to the patient. By using human DNA to produce proteins for medical use, such risks were greatly decreased, if not eliminated.

The first genetically engineered product approved for human use was human insulin. Insertion of the human insulin gene into bacteria was accomplished by the pioneer genetic engineering company Genentech. Following extensive testing and government approval, large-scale production of genetically engineered human insulin was carried out, with recombinant human insulin first marketed to diabetics in 1982. Today, genetically engineered human growth hormone, parathyroid hormone, and similar proteins have provided a new standard of care to individuals suffering from endocrine diseases.

The interferons also were among the first recombinant proteins produced for therapeutics. Interferons belong to a class of immune-system proteins called cytokines and are used to treat viral infections and some cancers, notably the virulent form of Kaposi's sarcoma common in patients with AIDS. Before the development of genetic engineering, it took laborious processing of thousands of units of human blood to obtain enough interferon, of somewhat impure quality, to treat a few patients. Genetic engineering enables the cost-effective production of vast quantities of very pure recombinant interferons.

Recombinant technology is used to produce a wide range of therapeutic substances. These include cytokines, interleukins, and monoclonal antibodies, all of which are used to fight certain viruses and cancers. Critical blood factors are now mass-produced through recombinant technology; these include clotting proteins such as factor VIII, used to treat bleeding disorders such as hemophilia; erythropoietin, which stimulates red blood cell production and is needed to combat anemia; and tissue plasminogen activator, a protein that helps dissolve the blood clots that block arteries during a heart attack or certain types of stroke.

Genetic engineering has also provided a means to produce safer vaccines. The first step is to identify the gene in a disease-causing virus that stimulates protective immunity. That gene is isolated and inserted into a vector molecule such as a harmless virus. The recombinant virus is used as a vaccine, producing immunity without exposing people to the disease-causing virus.

Recombinant DNA technology is also used in the prenatal diagnosis of inherited diseases. Restriction enzymes are used to cut the DNA of parents who may carry a gene for a congenital disorder. These fragments are compared with DNA from the fetus. In many situations the disease status of the fetus can be determined. This technique is used to detect a wide range of genetic disorders, including thalassemias, Huntington disease, cystic fibrosis, and Duchenne muscular dystrophy.

In gene therapy, scientists use vector molecules to insert a functional gene into the cells of individuals suffering from a disorder caused by a defective gene. Vector molecules containing a functional gene are inserted into a culture of the patient's own cells, which then deliver the inserted genes to the targeted diseased organs or tissues. The most commonly used vectors in gene therapy are viruses. In the target (human host) cell, the virus "unloads" the inserted gene, which then begins functioning, restoring the cell to a healthy state. Another method is to take a cell from the patient, use recombinant technology to remove the nonfunctional gene and replace it with a functional one, allow the cell to replicate, and then infuse the engineered cells directly into the patient. For

This girl suffers from cystic fibrosis, an inherited disease of the glands primarily affecting the digestive and respiratory systems. Scientists hope to treat the disease with gene therapy.

example, to treat the life-threatening deficiency of the immune system protein adenosine deaminase (ADA), scientists infuse cells from the patient's own blood into which researchers have inserted copies of the gene that directs production of ADA. Although there are still a number of challenges to overcome in developing gene therapy, it remains a research area of great promise.

GENETIC ENGINEERING IN INDUSTRY

Genetic engineering has been especially valuable for producing recombinant microorganisms that have a wide variety of industrial uses. Among the most important achievements have been the production of modified bacteria that devour hydrocarbons. These microbes are used to destroy oil slicks and to clean up sites contaminated with toxic wastes. Genetically engineered microbes are used to produce enzymes used in laundry detergents and contact lens solutions. Recombinant microbes also are used to make substances that can be converted to polymers such as polyester for use in bedding and other products.

GENETIC ENGINEERING IN AGRICULTURE

Genetic engineering has had a significant impact on agriculture. Scientists have used recombinant DNA to create crops with new attributes that improve crop yield or boost nutritional value. These crops are known as genetically modified organisms (GMOs). For example, genetic engineering was used to create "golden rice." This is a strain of white rice that had the gene for beta-carotene (which is a precursor of vitamin A) added to it, producing a nutrient-dense rice. It was engineered for use in developing countries where rice is a staple and vitamin-A deficiency is widespread. Scientists have also used generic engineering in ways that make agriculture more profitable. They have produced tomatoes with longer shelf lives, which means fewer of them go bad before they can be sold. New potato varieties that are resistant to pests, such as Columbia root-knot nematodes, and potato leaf roll virus make for more profitable potato crops.

These researchers are working with potato plants that have been genetically engineered to be more productive. Public opinion on such genetically modified organisms is divided.

The introduction and use of GMOs have been somewhat controversial. Several consumer groups and environmental groups have voiced reservations about the safety of GMOs and the products produced using them. So have certain government agencies and ecologists. However, it is unlikely that the use of genetic engineering in agriculture will be halted. Although GMOs are banned in some countries, the vast majority of the soybeans, cotton, and corn raised commercially in the United States are genetically modified.

BIOMECHANICS

Ideas and investigations relating to biomechanics date back at least to the Renaissance, when Italian physiologist and physicist Giovanni Alfonso Borelli first described the basis of muscular and skeletal dynamics. Research in biomechanics became more widely known in the 20th century.

Contemporary biomechanics is a multidisciplinary field that combines physical and engineering expertise with knowledge from the biological and medical sciences. There are multiple specialty areas in biomechanics, such as cardiovascular biomechanics, cell biomechanics, human movement biomechanics

HUMAN-FACTORS ENGINEERING

Human-factors engineering, also called ergonomics, is the science deal-ing with the application of information on physical and psychological characteristics to the design of devices and systems for human use.

The design of a complicated device, such as a space suit, presents intricate problems. A space suit is a complete miniature world, a self-contained environment that must supply everything needed for an astronaut's life, as well as comfort. The suit must provide a pressurized interior, without which an astronaut's blood would boil in the vacuum of space. The consequent pressure differential between the inside and the outside of the suit is so great that when inflated the suit becomes a distended, rigid, and unyielding capsule. Special joints were designed to give the astronaut as much free movement as possible. The best engineer-ing has not been able to provide as much flexibility of movement as is desirable; to compensate for that lack, attention has been directed toward the human-factors design of the tools and devices that an astronaut must use.

In addition to overcoming pressurization and movement problems, a space suit must provide oxygen; a system for removing excess products of respiration, carbon dioxide and water vapour; protection against extreme heat, cold, and radi-ation; protection for the eyes in an environment in which there is no atmosphere to absorb the sun's rays; facilities for speech communication; and facilities for the temporary storage of body wastes. This is such an imposing list of human requirements that an entire technology has been developed to deal with them and, indeed, with the provision of simulated environments and procedures for testing and evaluating space suits.

(in particular orthopedic biomechanics), occupational biomechanics, and sport biomechanics. As an example, sport biomechanics deals with performance improvement and injury prevention in athletes. In occupational biomechanics, biomechanical analysis is used to understand and optimize mechanical interaction of workers with the environment.

Biomechanics research has fueled a diverse range of advances, many of which affect daily human life. Development of the biomechanics of labour, for example, focused on increasing worker efficiency without sacrificing labour safety. It resulted in the design of new tools, furniture, and other elements of a working environment that minimize load on the worker's body. Another development was clinical biomechanics, which employs mechanical facts, methodologies, and mathematics to interpret and analyze typical and atypical human anatomy and physiology.

During World War I and World War II, there was significant focus on the development of prosthetic limbs for amputee veterans, which led to major progress in biomechanics and rehabilitation medicine. Work in that area focused on increasing the mechanical efficiency of orthopedic implants, such as those used for hip or knee replacements. A biomechanics research-based approach also helped contribute to improvements in walking devices designed for individuals with lower-leg amputation and children with cerebral palsy. The development of a new class of prosthetic feet that store and return mechanical energy during walking allowed for a reduction of metabolic expenditure in amputees and made it possible for individuals with amputation to participate in athletic activities. The biomechanically based design of assistive devices, such as wheelchairs, and the optimization of environmental elements, such as stairs, allowed individuals with disabilities to improve their mobility.

The applications of biomechanics are wide-ranging. Some examples include the use of biomechanical analysis in the design of implantable artificial prostheses, such as artificial hearts and small-diameter blood vessels; in the engineering of living tissues, such as heart valves and intervertebral discs; and in injury prevention related to vehicle accidents, including low-speed collisions involving minor soft-tissue injuries and high-speed collisions involving severe and fatal injuries.

BIOCHEMICAL ENGINEERING

Biochemical engineers develop practical applications of biochemistry, the study of the chemical substances and processes that occur in plants, animals, and microorganisms and of the changes they undergo during development and life. All chemical changes within the organism—either the degradation of substances, generally to gain necessary energy, or the buildup of complex molecules necessary for life processes—are collectively termed metabolism. These chemical changes depend on the action of organic catalysts known as enzymes, and enzymes, in turn, depend for their existence on the genetic apparatus of the cell. It is not surprising, therefore, that biochemistry enters into the investigation of chemical changes in disease, drug action, and other aspects of medicine, as well as in nutrition, genetics, and agriculture.

An early objective in biochemistry was to provide analytical methods for the determination of various blood constituents because it was felt that abnormal levels might indicate the presence of metabolic diseases. The clinical chemistry laboratory now has become a major investigative arm of the physician in the diagnosis and treatment of disease and is an indispensable unit of every hospital. Some of the older analytical methods directed toward diagnosis of common diseases are still the most commonly used—for example, tests for determining the levels of blood glucose, in diabetes; urea, in kidney disease; uric acid, in gout; and bilirubin, in liver and gallbladder disease. With development of the knowledge of enzymes, determination of certain enzymes in blood plasma has assumed diagnostic value, such as alkaline phosphatase, in bone and liver disease; acid phosphatase, in prostatic cancer; amylase, in pancreatitis; and lactate dehydrogenase and transaminase, in cardiac infarct. Electrophoresis of plasma proteins is commonly employed to aid in the diagnosis of various liver diseases and forms of cancer. Both electrophoresis and ultracentrifugation of serum constituents (lipoproteins) are used increasingly in the diagnosis and examination of therapy of atherosclerosis and heart disease. Many specialized and sophisticated methods have been introduced, and machines have been developed for the simultaneous automated analysis of many different blood constituents in order to cope with increasing medical needs.

Analytical biochemical methods have also been applied in the food industry to develop crops superior in nutritive value and capable of retaining nutrients during the processing and preservation of food. Research in this area is directed particularly to preserving vitamins as well as colour and taste, all of which may suffer loss if oxidative enzymes remain in the preserved food. Tests for enzymes are used for monitoring various stages in food processing.

Biochemical techniques have been fundamental in the development of new drugs. The testing of potentially useful drugs includes studies on experimental animals and man to observe the desired effects and also to detect possible toxic manifestations; such studies depend heavily on many of the clinical biochemistry techniques already described. Although many of the commonly used drugs have been developed on a rather empirical (trial-and-error) basis, an increasing number of therapeutic agents have been designed specifically as enzyme inhibitors to interfere with the metabolism of a host or invasive agent. Biochemical advances in the knowledge of the action of natural hormones and antibiotics promise to aid further in the development of specific pharmaceuticals.

SYNTHETIC BIOLOGY

Synthetic biology incorporates many different scientific techniques and approaches. The synthetic systems created may be used to generate products ranging from ethanol and drugs to complete synthetic organisms such as complex bacteria that can digest and neutralize toxic chemicals. Ideally, these customized synthetic biological systems and organisms would be much safer and less complicated than approaches based on the manipulation of naturally occurring biological entities. Synthetic systems and organisms would essentially operate like biological "factories" or "computers."

HISTORY OF SYNTHETIC BIOLOGY

One could consider the first scientist to have successfully conducted synthetic biology research to be Friedrich Wöhler, a German chemist who in 1828 applied ammonium chloride to silver isocyanate to produce urea, the main nitrogen-carrying compound found in the urine of mammals. In so doing, he synthesized an organic substance from inorganic matter. From then on, scientists routinely created organic matter through various conventional chemical processes.

In the 1970s scientists began to conduct experiments with genetic engineering and recombinant DNA technology, in which they modified the genetic code of wild-type (naturally occurring) bacteria by inserting single wild-type genes that could alter bacterial function. This technology led to the production of biologic drugs, agents made from proteins and other organic compounds produced by bacteria with recombinant DNA; one such compound is synthetic insulin. However, because genetic engineering uses existing genes and bacteria, it has technical limitations and is expensive.

In the early 1970s, paralleling developments in genetic engineering, scientists discovered ways to manufacture customized genes, which were built from scratch, or *de novo* (Latin for "anew"), one nucleotide (one unit of DNA) at a time. Throughout the 1980s and '90s and in the early 2000s, DNA synthesis technologies became increasingly time- and cost-efficient, thereby enabling steady advance and more ambitious experimentation. By manufacturing novel stretches of DNA, scientists have been able to efficiently create de novo organic compounds that are more complex than those that occur in nature and that are better suited for specific purposes.

ADVANCES IN SYNTHETIC BIOLOGY

In June 2007, scientists at the J. Craig Venter Institute (JCVI) in the United States took synthetic biology to a new level when they successfully transplanted the entire genome of one species of bacterium (*Mycoplasma mycoides*) into the cytoplasm of another (*Mycoplasma capricolum*), accomplishing the first full genome transplant. The new bacteria were completely devoid of their native genes and, after cell division, became phenotypically equivalent (similar in their observable characteristics) to *M. mycoides*.

In January 2008, JCVI scientists Daniel G. Gibson and Hamilton O. Smith successfully assembled a modified version of the genome of the bacterium *M. genitalium* from scratch. This was markedly different from the one-by-one gene modifications of recombinant DNA research, since numerous genes were linked together to create a new genome. The synthetic genome was only slightly different from the natural one; the slight differences kept the genome from becoming pathogenic (disease-causing) and also allowed it to be identified as artificial. The scientists dubbed this new version *M. genitalium*

JCVI-1.0. Having 582,970 base pairs, it was 10 times longer than any previously assembled genome. *M. genitalium* JCVI-1.0 was created from 101 custom-made, overlapping "cassettes," each of which was 5,000–7,000 nucleotides long. *M. genitalium* was chosen for the experiment because it is the simplest naturally occurring bacterium that can be grown in vitro (under laboratory conditions); its genome is made up of only 482 genes (plus 43 RNA-coding genes).

A scanning electron micrograph of cells of Mycoplasma mycoides JCVI-syn1.0, a synthetic bacterium created at the J. Craig Venter Institute.

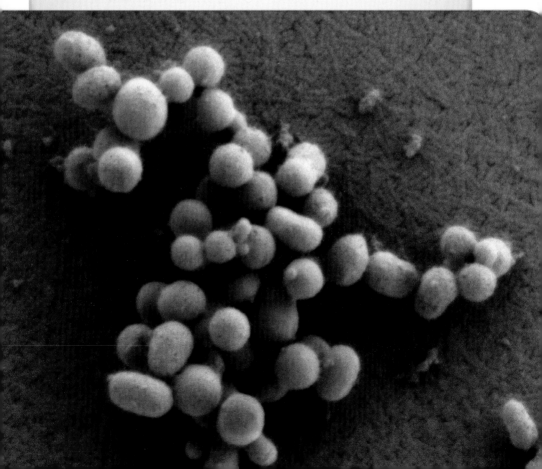

The scientists at JCVI hypothesized that about 100 more genes could be removed from the *M. genitalium* JCVI-1.0 genome without sacrificing its function (although they were not sure which 100 genes). A genome of approximately 381 genes is believed to be the minimum size necessary to sustain life. The researchers planned to create this abbreviated genome, which they would then insert into a cell, thereby creating an artificial life-form. They planned to call this life-form *M. laboratorium*, and they filed a patent application for it. *M. laboratorium* would be used as a chassis upon which other genes could be added to create customized bacteria for numerous purposes, including as new forms of fuel or as environmental cleaners, capable of removing pollutants from soil, air, or water.

In May 2010, JCVI researchers announced that they had created a 1.08-million-base-pair synthetic genome and inserted it into the cytoplasm of a bacterium, making the first functioning life-form with a synthetic genome. This genome was almost identical to the naturally occurring genome of *M. mycoides*, except that it had certain genetic "watermarks" to indicate its synthetic composition.

Another scientist prominent in the field of synthetic biology was American bioengineer Drew Endy, who founded the nonprofit BioBricks Foundation. Endy was developing a catalogue of information needed to synthesize basic biological parts, or "bricks," from DNA and other molecules. Other scientists and engineers were able to use this information to build whatever biological products they wanted, knowing that certain "bricks" would consistently carry out the same function in larger organic constructions. It was Endy's hope that the BioBricks would do for bioengineering what resistors and transistors did for electrical engineering. Still other scientists attempted to create synthetic DNA with an expanded genetic code that included new base pairs in addition to the naturally occurring pairs of A-T (adenine-thymine) and C-G (cytosine-guanine).

A variation on the theme of synthetic DNA entails the synthesis of nucleic acids that carry the natural base pairs of DNA but possess a backbone made with sugars other than deoxyribose. These molecules, known as xeno-nucleic acids (XNAs), cannot be replicated by the enzyme DNA polymerase, which catalyzes the synthesis of DNA. Instead, their replication requires specially engineered enzymes: The first that were capable of faithfully transcribing DNA into the desired XNA product were reported in 2012.

APPLICATIONS OF SYNTHETIC BIOLOGY

Many scientists suspect that synthetic biology will not only reveal new knowledge about the machinery of life but also bring about new biotechnological applications. Two major applications that are being pursued are biofuels and pharmaceuticals. For instance, researchers have been working on the synthetic manufacture of the antimalarial drug artemisinin, which is produced naturally in the sweet wormwood plant (*Artemisia annua*), a slow-growing species. By using the techniques of synthetic biology, scientists teased apart the plant's DNA sequences and protein pathways that produce artemisinin and combined them with yeast and bacteria. This increased the production of synthetic artemisinin by some 10 million times the output that was possible in the late 1990s.

Other scientists have gone beyond this "cell factory" approach, which is still similar to the work done with recombinant DNA, by trying to create new forms of bacteria that can destroy tumours. The Defense Advanced Research Projects Agency (DARPA) of the U.S. Department of Defense has experimented with the creation of biological computers, and other military scientists are trying to engineer proteins and gene products from scratch that will act as targeted vaccines or cures.

In the area of biofuels, scientists at numerous companies are trying to create microbes that can break down dense feedstocks (such as switchgrass) to produce biofuels; such feedstocks can be grown, processed, and burned in a way that is more efficient, less expensive, and environmentally sustainable relative to the fossil fuels that vehicles currently use.

American geneticist and biochemist J. Craig Venter led an effort to modify the genes of microbes to secrete oil. If successfully scaled up for commercial production, these organisms could serve as valuable sources of renewable energy.

RISK ASSESSMENT AND ETHICAL CONCERNS IN SYNTHETIC BIOLOGY

Synthetic biology is not without its risks. Like nearly all technologies, it can be used for good or for ill, and those ills can be intentional or accidental. However, there is some debate as to whether synthetic biology represents categorically different risks from those posed by other forms of biological research and genetic engineering. Both genetically engineered and synthetic organisms are capable of reproducing, mutating, evolving, and spreading through the environment, which makes them riskier than hazardous chemicals. But since the advent of genetic engineering in the 1970s, scientists have learned that artificial organisms designed for laboratory use are less well-suited for survival in the natural environment compared with naturally occurring organisms.

Synthetic biology does not add much to the threat of biological weapons, because DNA synthesis is an expensive process; there are less-expensive genetic engineering techniques that have been around for decades. The risk of accidents can be handled similarly to the way any potentially hazardous research is typically handled—through education, systems of accountability, record keeping, and possibly licensure or accreditation of scientists who do such research or handle such products. Nevertheless, there is concern over so-called "emergent properties," which could arise unexpectedly when de novo genes with no natural lineage enter the environment and interact with one another. This is especially risky for synthetic organisms that are designed for use outside the laboratory. Scientists and engineers will need to design organisms that remain stable; this could be achieved through efforts that prevent the organisms from being able to evolve new traits or that cause them to lose their designed traits. However, whereas it is relatively easy to predict what a synthetic organism will do in its intended environment, it is far more difficult to predict how it will evolve after multiple generations of exposure to environmental pressures or interaction with other organisms.

BIONICS

Bionics is the science of constructing artificial systems that have some of the characteristics of living systems. Mimicry of nature is an old idea. Many inventors have modeled machines after animals throughout the centuries. Copying from nature has distinct advantages. Most living creatures now on the Earth are the product of two billion years of evolution, and the construction of machines to work in an environment resembling that of living creatures can profit from this enormous experience. Although the easiest way may be thought to be direct imitation of nature, this is often difficult if not impossible, among other reasons because of the difference in scale. Bionics researchers have found that it is more advantageous to understand the principles of why things work in nature than to slavishly copy details.

The next step is the generalized search for inspiration from nature. Living beings can be studied from several points of view. Animal muscle is an efficient mechanical motor; solar energy is stored in a chemical form by plants with almost 100 percent efficiency; transmission of information within the nervous system is more complex than the largest telephone exchanges; problem solving by a human brain exceeds by far the capacity of the most powerful supercomputers. These exemplify the two main fields of bionics research—information processing and energy transformation and storage.

In the living world, energy is stored in the form of chemical compounds; its use always is accompanied by chemical reactions. Solar energy is stored by plants by means of complex chemical processes. The energy of muscular motion is derived from chemical changes. The light produced by such living organisms as mushrooms, glowworms, and certain fishes is of chemical origin. In every case the energy transformation is remarkably efficient compared with thermal engines.

A beginning is being made in understanding how these transformations take place in living material and the nature of the complex role played by living membranes. Perhaps some of the limitations of molecular complexity and fragility could be overcome in man-made artificial-energy machines and better results achieved than in natural membranes.

BIOINFORMATICS

Bioinformatics is the application of the techniques of informatics to biological data. Informatics, also known as information science, deals with the processes of storing and transferring information. It attempts to bring together concepts and methods from such varied disciplines as library science, computer science and engineering, linguistics, and psychology to develop techniques and devices to aid in the handling of information. In its early stages in the 1960s, information science was concerned primarily with applying the then-new computer technology to the processing and managing of documents. The applied computer technologies and theoretical studies of information science have since permeated many other disciplines. Computer science and engineering still tend to absorb its theory- and technology-oriented subjects, and management science tends to absorb information-systems subjects.

One of the primary applications of bioinformatics is in the study of the human genome, which consists of all of the approximately three billion base pairs of DNA that make up the entire set of chromosomes of the human organism. Bioinformatics has also proven a valuable tool for studying macromolecular structures, as well as analyzing the results of functional genomic experiments, which attempt to help us develop a better understanding of the functions of genes and the proteins that they are integral in making.

AGRICULTURAL ENGINEERING

Today, in light of increasing global population growth, many researchers point to biotechnology as a source of great promise for feeding the world. Bioengineers have introduced specific desirable genes into plants and animals that could endow crops and livestock with built-in insect resistance and herbicide tolerance. This science is also being used to make important global foods, like rice and cassava, more nutritious. This is critical, as vitamin deficiencies, particularly vitamin A and iron deficiencies, are prevalent across the developing world.

As competition for land increases and agricultural productivity peaks, agricultural research has extended to redesigning plants by genetic manipulation. This offers the hope for lessening the need for feed and fertilizer supplements. Additionally, disease resistance increasingly will be built into crops, which will also reduce chemical applications and conserve the quality of water and soil resources. Plants will be able to grow on arid land or in salt marshes. Almost any desired genetic change is possible.

Better control of plant and animal diseases and pests has aided the increase in agricultural output.

Inorganic chemical pesticides were generally used before 1945. Organic chemicals developed later include chlorinated hydrocarbons, such as toxaphene and benzene hexachloride. They also include organic phosphates, such as malathion and parathion. Scientists test each new chemical to be sure that no harmful residue will poison treated food plants. Environmental regulations in many countries also require testing to ensure that insecticides being used will not harm fish and wildlife. The combined use of minimal amounts of chemicals and of natural methods to control pests is called integrated pest management and is considered by many to be the most desirable control technique.

Researchers in the United States and around the world are currently investigating how best to manage such disease threats through the development of better diagnostic methods and vaccines and by exploring how biotechnology might someday endow livestock with built-in disease resistance.

Leaner beef and more nutritious eggs and fish, containing higher levels of healthful fatty acids, are being developed. Helping shed light on such projects is an increased knowledge of animals' genetic makeup. U.S. animal scientists and their public and private partners worldwide have mapped the genetic blueprint—or genome—of several animals already, including the cow, chicken, and honeybee. Honeybees are unsung heroes on our farmlands,

Monitoring natural resources and environmental conditions may be a part of an agricultural engineer's job. These agricultural engineers are inspecting a dry stream channel.

responsible for pollinating $15 billion worth of crops—mostly fruits, vegetables, and nuts—in the United States alone.

Agricultural engineers also find ways to lessen the environmental impact of agriculture. This may mean finding new ways to deal with the runoff from fertilizers and pesticides Finding environmentally appropriate uses for animal manure is another challenge. Agricultural engineers also concern themselves with developing agricultural techniques that deplete the soil less or require smaller amounts of water and other resources.

CHAPTER 6

ENVIRONMENTAL ENGINEERING

Environmental engineering is the development of processes and infrastructure for the water supply, the disposal of waste, and the control of pollution of all kinds. These endeavours protect public health by preventing disease transmission, and they preserve the quality of the environment by averting the contamination and degradation of air, water, and land resources.

Mathematical modeling and computer analysis are widely used to evaluate and design the systems required for such tasks. Chemical and mechanical engineers may also be involved in the process. Environmental engineering functions include applied research and teaching; project planning and management; the design, construction, and operation of facilities; the sale and marketing of environmental-control equipment; and the enforcement of environmental standards and regulations.

Projects in environmental engineering involve the treatment and distribution of drinking water; the collection, treatment, and disposal of wastewater; the control of air pollution and noise pollution; municipal solid-waste management and hazardous-waste management; the cleanup of hazardous-waste sites; and the preparation of environmental assessments, audits, and impact studies.

WATER TREATMENT

One concern of environmental engineering is the treatment of drinking water and waste water. Water pollutants may originate from point sources or from dispersed sources. A point-source pollutant is one that reaches water from a single pipeline or channel, such as a sewage discharge or outfall pipe. Dispersed sources are broad, unconfined areas from which pollutants enter a body of water. Surface runoff from farms, for example, is a dispersed source of pollution, carrying animal wastes, fertilizers, pesticides, and silt into nearby streams. Urban storm water drainage, which may carry sand and other gritty materials, petroleum residues from automobiles, and road de-icing chemicals, is also considered a dispersed source because of the many locations at which it enters local streams or lakes. Point-source pollutants are easier to control than dispersed-source pollutants, since they flow to a single location where treatment processes can remove them from the water. Such control is not usually possible over pollutants from dispersed sources, which cause a large part of the overall water pollution problem. Dispersed-source water pollution is best reduced by enforcing proper land-use plans and development standards.

General types of water pollutants include pathogenic organisms, oxygen-demanding wastes, plant nutrients, synthetic organic chemicals, inorganic chemicals, sediments, radioactive substances, oil, and heat. Sewage is the primary source of the first three types. Farms and industrial facilities are also sources of some of them. Sediment from eroded topsoil is considered a pollutant because it can damage aquatic ecosystems, and heat (particularly from power-plant cooling water) is considered a pollutant because of the adverse effect it has on dissolved oxygen levels and aquatic life in rivers and lakes.

It used to be said that, "the solution to pollution is dilution." When small amounts of sewage are discharged into a flowing body of water, a natural process of stream self-purification occurs. Densely populated communities generate such large quantities of sewage, however, that dilution alone does not prevent pollution. This makes it necessary to treat or purify wastewater to some degree before disposal.

The construction of centralized sewage treatment plants began in the late 19th and early 20th centuries, principally in the United Kingdom and the United States. Instead of discharging sewage directly into a nearby body of water, it was first passed through a combination of physical, biological, and chemical processes that removed some or most of the pollutants. Also beginning in the 1900s, new sewage-collection systems were designed to separate storm water from domestic wastewater, so that treatment plants did not become overloaded during periods of wet weather.

After the middle of the 20th century, increasing public concern for environmental quality led to broader and more stringent regulation of wastewater disposal practices. Higher levels of treatment were required. For example, pretreatment of industrial wastewater, with the aim of preventing toxic chemicals from interfering with the biological processes used at sewage treatment plants, often became a necessity. In fact, wastewater treatment technology advanced to the point where it became possible to remove virtually all pollutants from sewage. This was so expensive, however, that such high levels of treatment were not usually justified.

Wastewater treatment plants became large, complex facilities that required considerable amounts of energy for their operation. After the rise of oil prices in the 1970s, concern for energy conservation became a more important factor in the design of new

Wastewater treatment plants remove chemical and biological wastes from water. There are approximately 15,000 wastewater treatment facilities in the United States.

pollution control systems. Consequently, land disposal and subsurface disposal of sewage began to receive increased attention where feasible. Such "low-tech" pollution control methods not only might help to conserve energy but also might serve to recycle nutrients and replenish groundwater supplies.

AIR POLLUTION CONTROL

The techniques employed to reduce or eliminate the emission into the atmosphere of substances that can harm the environment or human health make up air pollution control. The control of air pollution is one of the principal areas of pollution control, along with wastewater treatment, solid-waste management, and hazardous-waste management.

Air is considered to be polluted when it contains certain substances in concentrations high enough and for durations long enough to cause harm or undesirable effects. These include adverse effects on human health, property, and atmospheric visibility. The atmosphere is susceptible to pollution from natural sources as well as from human activities. Some natural phenomena, such as volcanic eruptions and forest fires, may have not only local and regional effects but also long-lasting global ones. Nevertheless, only pollution caused by human activities, such as industry and transportation, is subject to mitigation and control.

Most air contaminants originate from combustion processes. During the Middle Ages the burning of coal for fuel caused recurrent air pollution problems in London and other large European cities. Beginning in the 19th century, in the wake of the Industrial Revolution, increasing use of fossil fuels intensified the severity and frequency of air pollution episodes. The advent of mobile sources of air pollution—i.e., gasoline-powered highway vehicles—had a tremendous impact on air quality problems in cities. It was not until the middle of the 20th century, however, that meaningful and lasting attempts were made to regulate or limit emissions of air pollutants from stationary and mobile sources and to control air quality on both regional and local scales.

The primary focus of air pollution regulation in industrialized countries has been on protecting ambient, or outdoor, air quality. This involves the control of a small number of specific "criteria" pollutants known to contribute to urban smog and chronic public health problems. The criteria pollutants include fine particulates, carbon monoxide, sulfur dioxide, nitrogen dioxide, ozone, and lead. Since the end of the 20th century, there also has been a recognition of the hazardous effects of trace amounts of many other air pollutants called "air toxics." Most air toxics are organic chemicals, comprising molecules that contain carbon, hydrogen, and other atoms. Specific emission regulations have been implemented against those pollutants. In addition, the long-term and far-reaching effects of the "greenhouse gases" on atmospheric chemistry and climate have been observed, and cooperative international efforts have been undertaken to control those pollutants. The greenhouse gases include carbon dioxide, chlorofluorocarbons (CFCs), methane, nitrous oxide, and ozone. In 2009 the U.S. Environmental Protection Agency ruled that greenhouse gases posed a threat to human health and could be subject to regulation as air pollutants.

The best way to protect air quality is to reduce the emission of pollutants by changing to cleaner fuels and processes. Pollutants not eliminated in this way must be collected or trapped by appropriate air-cleaning devices as they are generated and before they can escape into the atmosphere.

CONTROL OF PARTICULATES

Airborne particles can be removed from a polluted airstream by a variety of physical processes. Common types of equipment for collecting fine particulates include cyclones, scrubbers, electrostatic precipitators, and baghouse filters. Once collected, particulates adhere to each other, forming agglomerates that can readily be removed from the equipment and disposed of, usually in a landfill.

Because each air pollution control project is unique, it is usually not possible to decide in advance what the best type of particle-collection device (or combination of devices) will be; control systems must be designed on a case-by-case basis. Important particulate characteristics that influence the selection of collection devices include corrosivity, reactivity, shape, density, and especially size and size distribution (the range of different particle sizes in the airstream). Other design factors include airstream characteristics (e.g., pressure, temperature, and viscosity), flow rate, removal efficiency requirements, and allowable resistance to airflow. In general, cyclone collectors are often used to control industrial dust emissions and as pre-cleaners for other kinds of collection devices. Wet scrubbers are usually applied in the control of flammable or explosive dusts or mists from such sources as industrial and chemical processing facilities and hazardous-waste incinerators; they can handle hot airstreams and sticky particles. Electro-

THE EPA

The Environmental Protection Agency (EPA) is the agency of the U.S. government that sets and enforces national pollution-control standards. In 1970, in response to the welter of confusing, often ineffective environmental protection laws enacted by states and communities, President Richard Nixon created the EPA to fix national guidelines and to monitor and enforce them. Functions of three federal departments—of the Interior, of Agriculture, and of Health, Education, and Welfare—and of other federal bodies were transferred to the new agency. The EPA was initially charged with the administration of the Clean Air Act (1970), enacted to abate air pollution primarily from industries and motor vehicles; the Federal Environmental Pesticide Control Act (1972); and the Clean Water Act (1972), regulating municipal and industrial wastewater discharges and offering grants for building sewage-treatment facilities. By the mid-1990s the EPA was enforcing 12 major statutes, including laws designed to control uranium mill tailings; ocean dumping; safe drinking water; insecticides, fungicides, and rodenticides; and asbestos hazards in schools.

In the early 21st century the EPA's role expanded to address climate change. In 2007 the U.S. Supreme Court ruled in a case brought by the state of Massachusetts against the EPA that failure to regulate greenhouse gas emissions from motor vehicles was contrary to the requirements of the Clean Air Act. As a result, the EPA was given the responsibility to develop strategies to manage emissions of carbon dioxide and five other greenhouse gases. Stemming from this mandate, the EPA worked with the U.S. Department of Transportation to develop standards that would substantially increase vehicle fuel efficiency, and in 2011 it initiated a permitting program that placed the first limits on greenhouse gas emissions from power plants, refineries, and other large, stationary sources.

static precipitators and fabric-filter baghouses are often used at power plants.

A cyclone removes particulates by causing the dirty airstream to flow in a spiral path inside a cylindrical chamber. Dirty air enters the chamber from a tangential direction at the outer wall of the device, forming a vortex as it swirls within the chamber. The larger particulates, because of their greater inertia, move outward and are forced against the chamber wall. Slowed by friction with the wall surface, they then slide down the wall into a conical dust hopper at the bottom of the cyclone. The cleaned air swirls upward in a narrower spiral through an inner cylinder and emerges from an outlet at the top. Accumulated particulate dust is periodically removed from the hopper for disposal.

Cyclones are best at removing relatively coarse particulates. They can routinely achieve efficiencies of 90 percent for particles larger than about 20 micrometres (um; 20 millionths of a metre). By themselves, however, cyclones are not sufficient to meet stringent air quality standards. They are typically used as pre-cleaners.

Devices called wet scrubbers trap suspended particles by direct contact with a spray of water or

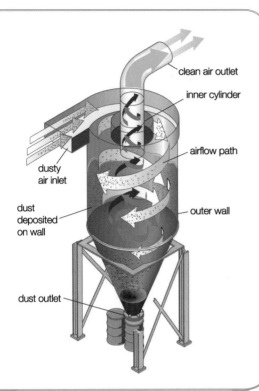

clean air outlet

inner cylinder

airflow path

dusty air inlet

dust deposited on wall

outer wall

dust outlet

Cyclone collectors are used to remove relatively coarse particulates from the air. Small cyclone devices are often installed to control pollution from mobile sources.

other liquid. In effect, a scrubber washes the particulates out of the dirty airstream as they collide with and are entrained by the countless tiny droplets in the spray. Several configurations of wet scrubbers are in use. In a spray-tower scrubber, an upward-flowing airstream is washed by water sprayed downward from a series of nozzles. In orifice scrubbers and wet-impingement scrubbers, the air and droplet mixture collides with a solid surface. Collision with a surface atomizes the droplets, reducing droplet size and thereby increasing total surface contact area. Venturi scrubbers achieve high relative velocities by injecting water into the throat of a venturi channel—a constriction in the flow path—through which particulate-laden air is passing at high speed.

Electrostatic precipitation is a commonly used method for removing fine particulates from airstreams. In an electrostatic precipitator, particles suspended in the airstream are given an electric charge as they enter the unit and are then removed by the influence of an electric field. The precipitation unit comprises baffles for distributing airflow, discharge and collection electrodes, a dust clean-out system, and collection hoppers. A high voltage of direct current (DC), as much as 100,000 volts, is applied to the discharge electrodes to charge the particles, which then are attracted to oppositely charged collection electrodes, on which they become trapped.

In a typical unit the collection electrodes comprise a group of large rectangular metal plates suspended vertically and parallel to each other inside a boxlike structure. There are often hundreds of plates having a combined surface area of tens of thousands of square metres. Rows of discharge electrode wires hang between the collection plates. The wires are given a negative electric charge, whereas the plates are grounded and thus become positively charged. Particles that stick to the collection plates are removed periodically when the plates are shaken, or "rapped."

One of the most efficient devices for removing suspended particulates is an assembly of fabric-filter bags, commonly called a baghouse. A typical baghouse comprises an array of long, narrow bags—each about 25 cm (10 inches) in diameter—that are suspended upside down in a large enclosure. Dust-laden air is blown upward through the bottom of the enclosure by fans. Particulates are trapped inside the filter bags, while the clean air passes through the fabric and exits at the top of the baghouse.

CONTROL OF GASES

Gaseous criteria pollutants, as well as volatile organic compounds (VOCs) and other gaseous air toxics, are controlled by means of three basic techniques: absorption, adsorption, and incineration (or combustion). These techniques can be employed singly or in combination. They are effective against the major greenhouse gases as well. In addition, a fourth technique, known as carbon sequestration, is in development as a means of controlling carbon dioxide levels.

In the context of air pollution control, absorption involves the transfer of a gaseous pollutant from the air into a contacting liquid, such as water. The liquid must be able either to serve as a solvent for the pollutant or to capture it by means of a chemical reaction. Wet scrubbers similar to those described above for controlling suspended particulates may be used for gas absorption. Gas absorption can also be carried out in packed scrubbers, or towers, in which the liquid is present on a wetted surface rather than as droplets suspended in the air. Cocurrent and cross-flow packed scrubber designs are also used for gas absorption. In the cocurrent design, both gas and liquid flow in the same direction—vertically downward through the scrubber. The cross-flow design, in which gas flows horizontally through the packing and liquid flows vertically downward, can operate with lower airflow resistance when high particulate levels are present.

Sulfur dioxide in flue gas from fossil-fuel power plants can be controlled by means of an absorption process called flue gas desulfurization (FGD). FGD systems may involve wet scrubbing or dry scrubbing. In wet FGD systems, flue gases are brought in contact with an absorbent, which can be either a liquid or a slurry of solid material. The sulfur dioxide dissolves in or reacts with the absorbent and becomes trapped in it. In dry FGD systems, the absorbent is dry pulverized lime or limestone; once absorption occurs, the solid particles are removed by means of baghouse filters.

Gas adsorption, as contrasted with absorption, is a surface phenomenon. The gas molecules are sorbed—attracted to and held—on the surface of a solid. Activated carbon (heated charcoal) is one of the most common adsorbent materials. It is very porous and has an extremely high ratio of surface area to volume. Activated carbon is particularly useful as an adsorbent for cleaning airstreams that contain VOCs and for solvent recovery and odour control. A properly designed carbon adsorption unit can remove gas with an efficiency exceeding 95 percent.

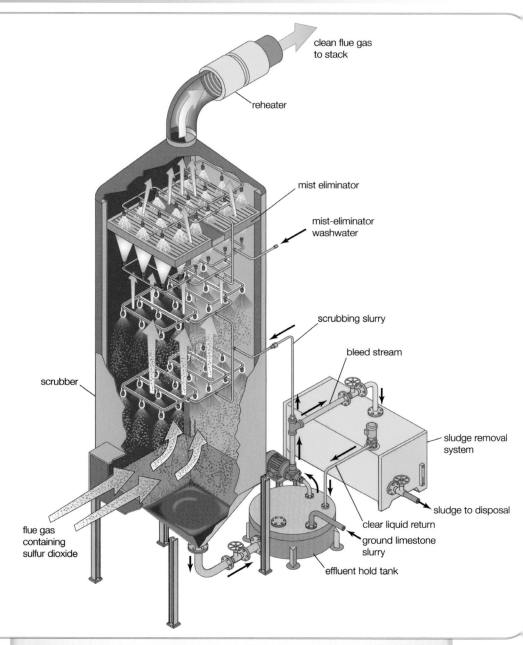

clean flue gas
to stack

reheater

mist eliminator

mist-eliminator
washwater

scrubbing slurry

bleed stream

scrubber

sludge removal
system

sludge to disposal

flue gas
containing
sulfur dioxide

clear liquid return

ground limestone
slurry

effluent hold tank

This wet scrubber uses a limestone slurry to remove sulfur dioxide from flue gas. In the limestone scrubbing process, sulfur dioxide reacts with limestone, forming calcium sulfite and carbon dioxide.

The process called incineration or combustion— chemically, rapid oxidation—can be used to convert VOCs and other gaseous hydrocarbon pollutants to carbon dioxide and water. Incineration of VOCs and hydrocarbon fumes usually is accomplished in a special incinerator called an afterburner. To achieve complete combustion, the afterburner must provide the proper amount of turbulence and burning time, and it must maintain a sufficiently high temperature. Sufficient turbulence, or mixing, is a key factor in combustion because it reduces the required burning time and temperature. A process called direct flame incineration can be used when the waste gas is itself a combustible mixture and does not need the addition of air or fuel.

The best way to reduce the levels of carbon dioxide in the air is to use energy more efficiently and to reduce the combustion of fossil fuels by using alternative energy sources (e.g., nuclear, wind, tidal, and solar power). In addition, carbon sequestration can be used to serve the purpose. Carbon sequestration involves the long-term storage of carbon dioxide underground, as well as on the surface of Earth in forests and oceans. Carbon sequestration in forests and oceans relies on natural processes such as forest growth. However, the clearing of forests for agricultural and other purposes (and also the pollution of oceans) diminishes natural carbon sequestration. Storing carbon dioxide underground—a technology under development that is also called geosequestration or carbon capture and storage—would involve pumping the gas directly into underground geologic "reservoir" layers. This would require the separation of carbon dioxide from power plant flue gases (or some other source)—a costly process.

SOLID-WASTE MANAGEMENT

Solid-waste management is the collecting, treating, and disposing of solid material that is discarded because it has served its purpose or is no longer useful. Improper disposal of municipal solid waste can create unsanitary conditions, and these conditions in turn can lead to pollution of the environment and to outbreaks of vector-borne disease—that is, diseases spread by rodents and insects. The tasks of solid-waste management present complex technical challenges. They also pose a wide variety of administrative, economic, and social problems that must be managed and solved.

A technological approach to solid-waste management began to develop in the latter part of the 19th century. Watertight garbage cans were first introduced in the United States, and sturdier vehicles were used to collect and transport wastes. A significant development in solid-waste treatment and disposal practices was marked by the construction of the first refuse incinerator in England in 1874. By the beginning of the 20th century, 15 percent of major American cities were incinerating solid waste. Even then, however, most of the largest cities were still using primitive disposal methods such as open dumping on land or in water.

Technological advances continued during the first half of the 20th century, including the development of garbage grinders, compaction trucks, and pneumatic collection systems. By mid-century, however, it had become evident that open dumping and improper incineration of solid waste were causing problems of pollution and jeopardizing public health. As a result, sanitary landfills were developed to replace the practice of open dumping and to reduce the reliance on waste incineration. In many countries waste was divided into two categories, hazardous and nonhazardous, and separate regulations were developed for their disposal. Landfills were designed and operated in a manner that minimized risks to public health and the environment. New refuse incinerators were designed to recover heat energy from the waste and were provided with extensive air pollution control devices to satisfy stringent standards of air quality. Modern solid-waste management plants in most developed countries now emphasize the practice of recycling and waste reduction at the source rather than incineration and land disposal.

Burning is a very effective method of reducing the volume and weight of solid waste. In modern incinerators the waste is burned inside a properly designed furnace under very carefully controlled conditions. The combustible portion of the waste combines with oxygen, releasing mostly carbon dioxide, water vapour, and heat. Incineration can reduce the volume of uncompacted waste by more than 90 percent, leaving an inert residue of ash, glass, metal, and other solid materials called bottom ash. The gaseous by-products of incomplete combustion, along with finely divided particulate material called fly ash, are carried along in the incinerator airstream. Fly ash includes cinders, dust, and soot. In order to remove fly ash and gaseous by-products before they are exhausted into the atmosphere, modern

West Contra Costa Sanitary Landfill, in Richmond, Calif. In sanitary landfills, thin layers of waste are compacted to form refuse cells, which are covered with a soil each evening.

incinerators must be equipped with extensive emission control devices. Such devices include fabric baghouse filters, acid gas scrubbers, and electrostatic precipitators. Bottom ash and fly ash are usually combined and disposed of in a landfill. If the ash is found to contain toxic metals, it must be managed as a hazardous waste.

Another method of treating municipal solid waste is composting, a biological process in which the organic portion of refuse is allowed to decompose under carefully controlled conditions. Microbes metabolize the organic waste material and reduce its volume by as much as 50 percent. The stabilized product is called compost or humus. It resembles potting soil in texture and odour and may be used as a soil conditioner or mulch. Composting offers a method of processing and recycling both garbage and sewage sludge in one operation. As more stringent environmental rules and siting constraints limit the use of solid-waste incineration and landfill options, the application of composting is likely to increase. The steps involved in the process include sorting and separating, size reduction, and digestion of the refuse.

Land disposal is the most common management strategy for municipal solid waste. Refuse can be safely deposited in a sanitary landfill, a disposal site that is carefully selected, designed, constructed, and operated to protect the environment and public health. One of the most important factors relating to landfilling is that the buried waste never comes in contact with surface water or groundwater. Engineering design requirements include a minimum distance between the bottom of the landfill and the seasonally high groundwater table. Most new landfills are required to have an impermeable liner or barrier at the bottom, as well as a system of groundwater-monitoring wells. Completed landfill sections must be capped with an impermeable cover to keep precipitation or surface runoff away from the buried waste. Bottom and cap liners may be made of flexible plastic membranes, layers of clay soil, or a combination of both.

Separating, recovering, and reusing components of solid waste that may still have economic value is called recycling. One type of recycling is the recovery and re-use of heat energy. Composting can also be considered a recycling process, since it reclaims the organic parts of solid waste for reuse as mulch or soil conditioner. Still other waste materials have potential for reuse. These include paper, metal, glass, plastic, and rubber.

HAZARDOUS-WASTE MANAGEMENT

The collection, treatment, and disposal of waste material that, when improperly handled, can cause substantial harm to human health and safety or to the environment is hazardous-waste management. Hazardous wastes can take the form of solids, liquids, sludges, or contained gases, and they are generated primarily by chemical production, manufacturing, and other industrial activities.

They may cause damage during inadequate storage, transportation, treatment, or disposal operations. Improper hazardous-waste storage or disposal frequently contaminates surface and groundwater supplies. People living in homes built near old and abandoned waste disposal sites may be in a particularly vulnerable position. In an effort to remedy existing problems and to prevent future harm from hazardous wastes, governments closely regulate the practice of hazardous-waste management.

Hazardous wastes are classified on the basis of their biological, chemical, and physical properties. These properties generate materials that are either toxic, reactive, ignitable, corrosive, infectious, or radioactive.

Toxic wastes are poisons, even in very small or trace amounts. They may have acute effects, causing death or violent illness, or they may have chronic effects, slowly causing irreparable harm. Some are carcinogenic, causing cancer after many years of exposure. Others are mutagenic, causing major biological changes in the offspring of exposed humans and wildlife.

Reactive wastes are chemically unstable and react violently with air or water. They cause explosions or form toxic vapours. Ignitable wastes burn at relatively low temperatures and may cause an immediate fire hazard. Corrosive wastes include strong acidic or alkaline substances. They destroy solid material and living tissue upon contact, by chemical reaction. Infectious wastes include used bandages, hypodermic needles, and other materials from hospitals or biological research facilities.

Radioactive wastes emit ionizing energy that can harm living organisms. Because some radioactive materials can persist in the environment for many thousands of years before fully decaying, there is much concern over the control of these wastes. However, the handling and disposal of radioactive material is not a responsibility of local municipal government. Because of the scope and complexity of the problem, the management of radioactive waste—particularly nuclear fission waste—is usually considered an engineering task separate from other forms of hazardous-waste management.

Hazardous waste generated at a particular site often requires transport to an approved treatment, storage, or disposal facility (TSDF). Because of potential threats to public safety and the environment, transport is given special attention by governmental agencies. In addition to the occasional accidental spill, hazardous waste has, in the past, been intentionally spilled or abandoned at random locations in a practice known as "midnight dumping." This practice has been greatly curtailed by the enactment of laws that require proper labeling, transport, and tracking of all hazardous wastes.

Several options are available for hazardous-waste management. The most desirable is to reduce the quantity of waste at its source or to recycle the materials for some other productive use. Nevertheless, while reduction and recycling are desirable options, they are not regarded as the final remedy to the problem of hazardous-waste disposal. There will always be a need for treatment and for storage or disposal of some amount of hazardous waste.

Hazardous waste can be treated by chemical, thermal, biological, and physical methods. Chemical methods include ion exchange, precipitation, oxidation and reduction, and neutralization. Among thermal methods is high-temperature incineration, which not only can detoxify certain organic wastes but also can destroy them. Special types of thermal equipment are used for burning waste in either solid, liquid, or sludge form. These include the fluidized-bed incinerator, multiple-hearth furnace, rotary kiln, and liquid-injection incinerator. One problem posed by hazardous-waste incineration is the potential for air pollution.

Biological treatment of certain organic wastes, such as those from the petroleum industry, is also an option. One method used to treat hazardous waste biologically is called landfarming. In this technique the waste is carefully mixed with surface soil on a suitable tract of land. Microbes that can metabolize the waste may be added, along with nutrients. In some cases a genetically engineered species of bacteria is used. Food or forage crops are not grown on the same site. Microbes can also be used for stabilizing hazardous wastes on previously contaminated sites; in that case the process is called bioremediation.

The chemical, thermal, and biological treatment methods outlined above change the molecular form of the waste material. Physical treatment, on the other hand, concentrates, solidifies, or reduces the volume of the waste. Physical processes include evaporation, sedimentation, flotation, and filtration. Yet another process is solidification, which is achieved by encapsulating the waste in concrete, asphalt, or plastic. Encapsulation produces a solid mass of material that is resistant to leaching. Waste can also be mixed with lime, fly ash, and water to form a solid, cementlike product.

Hazardous wastes that are not destroyed by incineration or other chemical processes need to be disposed of properly. For most such wastes, land disposal is the ultimate destination, although it is not an attractive practice, because of the inherent environmental risks involved. Two basic methods of land disposal include landfilling and underground injection. Prior to land disposal, surface storage or containment systems are often employed as a temporary method.

Disposal of hazardous waste in unlined pits, ponds, or lagoons poses a threat to human health and environmental quality. Many such uncontrolled disposal sites were used in the past and have been abandoned. Depending on a determination of the level of risk, it may

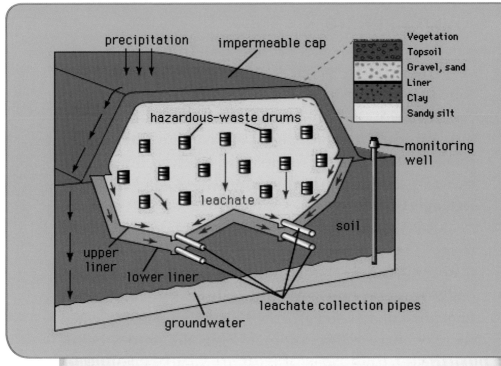

Hazardous wastes must be deposited in secure landfills, which provide at least 10 feet (3 m) of separation between the bottom of the landfill and the underlying bedrock or groundwater table.

be necessary to remediate those sites. In some cases, the risk may require emergency action. In other instances, engineering studies may be required to assess the situation thoroughly before remedial action is undertaken.

One option for remediation is to completely remove all the waste material from the site and transport it to another location for treatment and proper disposal. This so-called off-site solution is usually the most expensive option. An alternative is on-site remediation, which reduces the production of leachate and lessens the chance of groundwater contamination. On-site remediation may include temporary removal of the hazardous waste, construction of a secure landfill on the same site, and proper replacement of the waste. It may also include treatment of any contaminated soil or groundwater. Treated soil may be replaced on-site and treated groundwater returned to the aquifer by deep-well injection.

A less costly alternative is full containment of the waste. This is done by placing an impermeable cover over the hazardous-waste site and by blocking the lateral flow of groundwater with subsurface cutoff walls. It is possible to use cutoff walls for this purpose when there is a natural layer of impervious soil or rock below the site. The walls are constructed around the perimeter of the site, deep enough to penetrate to the impervious layer. They can be excavated as trenches around the site without moving or disturbing the waste material. The trenches are filled with a bentonite clay slurry to prevent their collapse during construction, and they are back-filled with a mixture of soil and cement that solidifies to form an impermeable barrier. Cutoff walls thus serve as vertical barriers to the flow of water, and the impervious layer serves as a barrier at the bottom.

CONCLUSION

Bioengineers have made many life-changing advances in recent years, and their accomplishments keep piling up. There's every reason to believe that breakthroughs in the field of bioengineering will continue in the years to come. The field itself will keep evolving as well, incorporating new perspectives, technologies, techniques, knowledge, and approaches. New subfields will come into being and maybe eventually spin off into full-fledged fields of their own.

While bioengineers have developed ingenious solutions to many problems with a medical and biological basis, plenty of challenges remain. These include everything from finding better methods for drug delivery to curing paralysis using neural engineering to developing microbial fuel cells (which produce energy from microbes such as bacteria).

Bioengineers are also exploring areas such as brain-computer interfaces, also known as mind-machine interfaces, which enable direct communication between a human mind and a device. They could be used to treat illnesses such as Alzheimer disease or amyotrophic lateral sclerosis (ALS), to communicate with patients who are incapable of speech, and to jolt tired drivers awake when they drift off to sleep at the wheel.

A new process called high-intensity focused ultrasound, or HIFU, uses narrowly focused ultrasonic waves. It is being used to treat uterine fibroids, which are noncancerous tumours that appear on the uterus. There are hopes that HIFU may also be a viable treatment for certain cancers, with clinical trials underway.

It's exciting to think what developments in bioengineering the future holds. The one thing we can be sure of is that bioengineers will continue to push the frontiers of human capability.

AMINO ACID Any one of many acids that occur naturally in living things and that include some which form proteins.

BIOMATERIAL A natural or synthetic material (as a metal or polymer) that is suitable for introduction into living tissue, especially as part of a medical device (as an artificial joint).

CARDIAC Of, relating to, situated near, or acting on the heart.

CHROMOSOME Any of the rod-shaped or threadlike DNA-containing structures of cellular organisms that are located in the nucleus of eukaryotes, are usually ring-shaped in prokaryotes (as bacteria), and contain all or most of the genes of the organism.

DEOXYRIBONUCLEIC ACID (DNA) Any of various nucleic acids that are usually the molecular basis of heredity, are constructed of a double helix held together by hydrogen bonds between purine and pyrimidine bases which project inward from two chains containing alternate links of deoxyribose and phosphate, and that in eukaryotes are localized chiefly in cell nuclei.

DIAGNOSTICS The art or practice of identifying a disease, illness, or problem by examining someone or something.

DYNAMICS A branch of mechanics that deals with forces and their relation primarily to the motion but sometimes also to the equilibrium of bodies.

ELECTRODE One of the two points through which electricity flows into or out of a battery or other device.

ENZYME Any of numerous complex proteins that are produced by living cells and catalyze specific biochemical reactions at body temperatures.

HORMONE A natural substance that is produced in the body and that influences the way the body grows or develops.

ISOTOPE Any one of various forms in which the atoms of a chemical element can occur.

METABOLISM The chemical processes by which a plant or an animal uses food, water, etc., to grow and heal and to make energy.

ORTHOPEDICS A branch of medicine concerned with the correction or prevention of deformities, disorders, or injuries of the skeleton and associated structures (as tendons and ligaments).

PHOTODETECTOR Any of various devices for detecting and measuring the intensity of radiant energy.

PIEZOELECTRICITY Electricity or electric polarity due to pressure especially in a crystalline substance (as quartz).

POLYMER A chemical compound that is made of small molecules that are arranged in a simple repeating structure to form a larger molecule.

PROSTHESIS An artificial device that replaces a missing or injured part of the body.

PROTEIN Any of various naturally occurring extremely complex substances that consist of amino-acid residues joined by peptide bonds; contain the elements carbon, hydrogen, nitrogen, oxygen, usually sulfur, and occasionally other elements (as phosphorus or iron); and include many essential biological compounds (as enzymes, hormones, or antibodies).

RADIOACTIVITY The property possessed by some elements (as uranium) or isotopes (as carbon 14) of spontaneously emitting energetic particles (as electrons or alpha particles) by the disintegration of their atomic nuclei.

RADIOGRAPHY The process of taking a photograph of the inside of a person's body by using X-rays.

RECOMBINATION The formation by the processes of crossing-over and independent assortment of new combinations of genes in progeny that did not occur in the parents.

STEM CELL An unspecialized cell that gives rise to differentiated cells.

SYNTHESIS The production of a substance by combining simpler substances through a chemical process.

THERMOREGULATION The maintenance of a particular temperature of the living body.

TOMOGRAPHY A method of producing a three-dimensional image of the internal structures of a solid object (as the human body or the Earth) by the observation and recording of the differences in the effects on the passage of waves of energy impinging on those structures.

BIOENGINEERING

Several of the major branches of bioengineering are treated in the following reference works: Richard Skalak and Stu Chien (eds.), *Handbook of Bioengineering* (1987); Jacob Kline (ed.), *Handbook of Biomedical Engineering* (1988); A. Edward Profio, *Biomedical Engineering* (1993); R.H. Brown (ed.), *CRC Handbook of Engineering in Agriculture*, 3 vol. (1988); Bernard Atkinson and Ferda Mavituna, *Biochemical Engineering and Biotechnology Handbook*, 2nd ed. (1991); Wesley E. Woodson, Barry Tillman, and Peggy Tillman, *Human Factors Design Handbook: Information and Guidelines for the Design of Systems, Facilities, Equipment, and Products for Human Use*, 2nd ed. (1992); Mark S. Sanders and Ernest J. McCormick, *Human Factors in Engineering and Design*, 7th ed. (1993); Alphonse Chapanis, *Human Factors in Systems Engineering* (1996); Robert A. Corbitt (ed.), *Standard Handbook of Environmental Engineering* (1990); P. Aarne Vesilind, J. Jeffrey Pierce, and Ruth F. Weiner, *Environmental Engineering*, 3rd ed. (1994); and James R. Pfafflin and Edward N. Ziegler (eds.), *Encyclopedia of Environmental Science and Engineering*, 3rd ed., rev. and updated, 2 vol. (1992).

MATERIALS SCIENCE

Robert A. Fuller and Jonathan J. Rosen, "Materials for Medicine," *Scientific American*, 255(4):118–125 (October 1986), offers an overview of the subject. S.A. Barenberg, "Abridged Report of the Committee to Survey the

Needs and Opportunities for the Biomaterials Industry,"
Journal of Biomedical Materials Research, 22(12):1267–92
(December 1988), surveys the applications of materials in
medicine and highlights projected areas of clinical need.
Joon Bu Park, *Biomaterials Science and Engineering* (1984),
provides a qualitative university-level introduction
to the field of biomaterials. Michael Szycher (ed.), *Biocompatible Polymers, Metals, and Composites* (1983), is a
collection of detailed review articles that covers materials in medicine and biocompatibility and contains a
pragmatic assessment of clinical and commercial
aspects, including how to sterilize and package biomaterials. Harry R. Allcock and Frederick W. Lampe,
Contemporary Polymer Chemistry, 2nd ed. (1990), is
a basic textbook of polymer science, providing a
university-level introduction to synthesis and characterization of polymers, including biomedical polymers.
Advanced biomaterials texts with emphasis on research
include Michael Szycher (ed.), *High Performance Biomaterials: A Comprehensive Guide to Medical and Pharmaceutical
Applications* (1991), research articles covering orthopedic
and cardiovascular biomaterials as well as most other
areas of materials in medicine; Joseph D. Andrade (ed.),
Surface and Interfacial Aspects of Biomedical Polymers, vol.
1, *Surface Chemistry and Physics* (1985), articles on surface characterization methods applied to biomaterials,
including a quantitative presentation of the interactions of blood components (especially proteins) with
biomaterial surfaces; Howard P. Greisler, *New Biologic
and Synthetic Vascular Prostheses* (1991), a biological per-
spective on blood interactions, wound healing, and

tissue integration with biomaterials and surface modified materials; D.F. Williams, *Blood Compatibility*, 2 vol. (1987), detailed review articles covering blood interactions with biomaterials and prosthetic devices and methods of modifying the surface of biomaterials; and H.L. Goldsmith and V.T. Turitto, "Rheological Aspects of Thrombosis and Hemostasis: Basic Principles and Applications," *Thrombosis and Haemostasis*, 55(3):415–435 (1986), a detailed and quantitative review article that describes and models blood flow and rheology in the vascular system, including the effects of different blood components.

ENVIRONMENTAL ENGINEERING

Jerry A. Nathanson, *Basic Environmental Technology: Water Supply, Waste Management, and Pollution Control*, 5th ed. (2008); and J. Jeffrey Peirce, P. Arne Vesilind, and Ruth Weiner, *Environmental Pollution and Control*, 4th ed. (1997), cover a variety of topics on environmental engineering and pollution control for a nontechnical audience. William P. Cunningham, Mary Ann Cunningham, and Barbara Woodworth Saigo, *Environmental Science: A Global Concern*, 9th ed. (2007), provides broad coverage of fundamental topics in environmental science, with a focus on biological aspects.